MY PROMISE HAS A PROBLEM

Danny Gardner

KNIGHTDALE, NC

Copyright © 2016 by **Danny Gardner**

All rights reserved. No part of this publication may be reproduced, distributed or transmitted in any form or by any means, without prior written permission.

Danny Gardner/Rain Publishing, LLC
PO Box 702
Knightdale, NC 27545
www.rainpublishing.com

My Promise Has a Problem/ Danny Gardner. -- 1st ed.
ISBN 978-0-9962421-5-8

Dedication

I would like to dedicate this book to my grandparents, the late Queen Esther Gardner and Johnnie Thrower. Although you have gone on to be with the Lord, all the good that you sowed into me as a child has now paid off. Thank You! I would also like to dedicate this book to my godmother, Mrs. Juanita Gardner. You were a Godsend in my life and I would not be where I am today if God, at that point in time, hadn't sent you to be a mother to me. I want to say thank you and I love you very dearly.

Acknowledgments

I want to thank my church family at Greater Judah Deliverance Ministries for all your love, commitment, and encouragement. Thank you to all the pastors and leaders who have poured into my life and helped make me the man God I am today. Thank you!

A special thanks to my loving wife, Sylvia Gardner, who is my best friend, lover, and companion. Without you I couldn't have done this - I Love You more than I could ever express in words. I can't forget my children: Dantrell, Naigel, and Michael. Thank you for loving me, too.

CONTENTS

Save Me from the Darkness 1
Loss of Innocence 5
Economic Hardship 11
Troubles at School 15
The Rejected Dreamer 23
Learning about Family 29
Struggling with School Work 33
Cycle of Addiction 37
Unexpected Pressures 43
Rock Bottom 47
Trouble with Women 53
A New Season 57
The Soft Tugging 61
An Encounter with the Savior 67
Losing My Grandfather 75
A New Aspect of Ministry 85
A Date with Destiny 91
Settling Into Marriage 99
When the Storms Rise 107
Problems with Posterity 111
Walking in Purpose 117

Prologue

Psalm 139:13-16 "For You formed my inward parts; You wove me in my mother's womb. I will give thanks to You, for I am fearfully and wonderfully made; Wonderful are Your works, and my soul knows it very well. My frame was not hidden from You, when I was made in secret, and skillfully wrought in the depths of the earth; Your eyes have seen my unformed substance; and in Your book were all written the days that were ordained for me, when as yet there was not one of them."

Often, the thought may enter our minds, "Does God have a purpose specifically for me?" The answer to that question is: *Yes!* God does have a purpose for your existence. As David expressed in the scripture above, the Lord made us wonderfully and even before that, He ordained our lives! So, we can be assured that as His children, His plans for each of us are sure and unique.

As David could also attest to, God's ordering of every step is not a perfectly smooth and easy journey. For some of us, God has given us specific promises that are not within reach and not easily obtainable. My firm belief is that whenever God gives you a promise, He also gives you problems equal to, or greater than the promise, to mold you, mature you, test your faith, and keep you cognizant and dependent on Him. We see in the bible that people often faced great difficulties before God's promise would come into fruition in their lives. Does that mean that God wasn't with them and isn't with us? It is quite the contrary! He allows us to go through troubles, tests, heartaches, headaches, and extreme lows in our lives to also prove to us that He is with us. He said in His word that **"He would never leave us nor would he forsake us" (Hebrews 13:5).**

David is a great example of someone who the Lord destined for great things but whose life was plagued with problems as God worked out His plan. In 1 Samuel 16, the prophet and judge of the nation, Samuel, bypassed all of David's older brothers and anointed his head with oil, representing God's choosing of him as Israel's next king. From that moment, it took over forty years for David to ascend to the throne. *Forty years!* Not only was that wait extremely long, but it was met with treacherous and sorrowful times.

Soon after David's initial interaction with Samuel, it became apparent to King Saul that the Spirit of the Lord was now with David, and Saul's jealousy led him to relentlessly conspire against and pursue David.

Psalm 59: 1-5 "Deliver me from mine enemies, O my God: defend me from them that rise up against me. Deliver me from the workers of iniquity, and save me from bloody men. For, lo, they lie in wait for my soul: the mighty are gathered against me; not for my transgression, nor for my sin, O Lord. They run and prepare themselves without my fault: awake to help me, and behold. Thou therefore, O Lord God of hosts, the God of Israel, awake to visit all the heathen: be not merciful to any wicked transgressors. Selah."

For many of those years, David had to hide in caves, on the run from the king. David even joined up with the Philistines, the very enemy he conquered that caused Saul's initial jealousy of his growing fame. All the while, David honored Saul, sparing his life on more than one occasion when he could have killed Saul and taken the throne on his own terms. But David would wait on the Lord to fulfill His promises in His way.

Saul's death still did not signal an easy road for David. Jonathan, David's kindred spirit and Saul's son, died along with the fallen king. David couldn't mourn this loss for long because his ascension to the throne was filled with more bloodshed. He was crowned king of Judah, but he did not have Israel and it was a long battle to gain that throne and unite the kingdom again. When things seemed to have settled, David desired to do something for the Lord – build a permanent temple. The Lord told him, "No," but then gave him a promise (covenant) that would be for his son and for generations after. As Hebrews 11 lets us know, as it chronicles the heroes of faith, many times God's promises are bigger than us and go beyond our lifetimes.

In all the fluctuations we see in David's life, with all the problems that he faced, God's promises remained sure. In fact, God used every problem to further His plan. And in the case of David, we know God's plan wasn't thwarted because we have a Savior in Jesus Christ! God's promise to David was that the Messiah would be His descendant and will reign on his throne forever! There are many other characters in the bible that shared difficult circumstances in the outworking of God's promises, but none as visible as David. Not only do we get his story, but through the Psalms, we get to understand his emotions, his attitude towards the Lord, and his belief that God would fulfill His plan for his life.

In the same way that David bore his soul as a testimony, I am sharing my life with you through this book. As you will see, my life has been filled with every form of darkness and wickedness to keep me from the promise God has set before me. It is not easy to lay myself bare, but I know that it will encourage someone else. If you have experienced difficulties in your past, don't give up! If you are going through storms in your life and feel like you can't see your way through, just hold on! The pathway is not perfect, but the promise is **real.** Don't trust in your timing to determine the truthfulness of the promise. You and I must trust in the One who gives the promise. His track record is flawless.

Part I

CHAPTER ONE

Save Me from the Darkness

> *And though this world, with devils filled, should threaten to undo us, we will not fear, for God hath willed his truth to triumph through us.*[i]

I would often pray and ask, "Why is this happening to me?" but received no answer. My life early on had taken some harsh twists. As a baby I was given to my grandparents, who were not my blood-relatives, they were my stepfather's parents. I was named after my stepfather, who constantly reminded me he wasn't my *real* father. He would curse me and call me derogatory names because of my light complexion. I couldn't help that I didn't have the darker brown skin tones of my family and community, and I developed a hatred for Caucasians because of the mental assault that was being waged on me daily. I was angry, **very** angry, and I was extremely lonely.

Since I was often by myself, demons presented themselves as my friends. That's right - *Demons*. Let's be realistic, no demon is a human being's friend; it's quite the opposite. *2 Corinthians 6:14 says, "for what fellowship hath righteousness with unrighteousness? and what communion hath light with darkness?"* But every day, two demons by the name of Jiff and John would manifest themselves as my friends and they would actually play ball with me in the hallway of my grandfather's home. As time passed, the visits became more frequent and my level of trust for them increased. They convinced me that Satan was God and I began, as a young child, to confess that Satan was God. The way that evil was twisted in my mind was unreal. I remember my neighbor asking me one day, "Who are you?" I replied, "I am Satan."

There was one night in particular, the demons walked in my bedroom and began to choke me while lifting me off the bed. I screamed for my grandfather and immediately they left. Shortly after this, the torment became more intense. I learned the demons thrive off fear! The more afraid I was, the more they would magnify themselves and try to scare me. I was always afraid to be alone because these beings would manifest regularly. I would be playing in the hallway and doors would open and close by themselves. I would hear the demons talking and their voices would increase in correspondence to my fear.

The fear wasn't new. When I was four, I would sense something that stood at my bedroom door and watched me every night. Every time I would tell my grandmother there was someone standing there, this demonic being would step back. This went on night after night. I was not always able to see this demonic being, but I can remember feeling its presence when I would get up each day. *Can you imagine being a child, seeing demonic activity and having no one understand or believe you?* As time went on I began to see greater manifestations of demonic beings. I would try to explain to my grandparents what I was seeing, but they would shun me. For a while, my grandmother thought something was wrong with me, but what she did not understand is the devil was at work, trying to hinder God's plan.

Lessons from the Journey

I had an extremely hard time dealing with the high level of spiritual attack I faced as a child. Now that I am older and know the Lord, I understand that these difficulties were a part of God's plan. There are many times in the Psalms that we see David asking for God's deliverance from his enemies. Then we see a passage like ***Psalm 23:4-5*** when he says ***"Yea, though I walk through the valley of the shadow of death, I will fear no evil; For You are with me...You prepare a table before me in the presence of my enemies."*** Even though there were times of fear and doubt, David ultimately understood who was in control of all the darkness going on. The bible also tells us in ***Romans 8:28***, ***"And we know that all things work together for good to those who love God, to those who are the called according to His purpose."*** And then the apostle Paul goes on to say in verse 31, ***"If God is for us, who can be against us?"*** Because we belong to Christ, NOTHING has dominion over us! Although the enemy was the culprit behind these attacks, God allowed them. So know this, that if Satan is attacking you, God has allowed it. Nothing we will encounter will take God by surprise! God knows our beginning from our end, so whatever you are going through, praise God that He already made provision for your deliverance!

CHAPTER TWO

Loss of Innocence

> *Psalm 18:4-5 "The pangs of death surrounded me, And the floods of ungodliness made me afraid. The sorrows of Sheol surrounded me; The snares of death confronted me."*

The spiritual issue I was dealing with from a young age was enough. Feeling misunderstood by my grandparents was enough. My growing anger because I looked different, and being treated harshly because of it, was enough. But there were more problems coming my way. One day my stepfather took me to a house, which was in the country part of Ayden, North Carolina, and he and another man had sex with a woman in a separate room. I could hear them plainly and I remember thinking it was gross. After a while he called me in the room and told me to touch her. I did not want to do it because something inside of me felt it was wrong. When I told him I wouldn't do it, he immediately called me a faggot and pushed me around. He made me touch her vagina and then pushed me down to the floor. They all laughed and called me many names and the rage inside me grew more as a result. While they laughed and poked fun at me, I cried. And the more I cried, the more my stepfather called me a faggot and the more my innocence was scarred.

Day after day I was called a faggot and became angrier. I would wait until my stepfather fell asleep after coming in extremely drunk, then I would throw cold water on him and run. I even turned more and more to the powers of darkness, asking Satan to kill him. My stepfather not only hurt me, but I saw so much evil in him. He would return home, drunk, and beat my grandmother and other women he dated. I often told myself that I would never be that way. I would cry many nights and ask God, even though I thought he was Satan, "Please kill me and take me away from this mess." The life I had didn't seem worth it. I only wanted a father that loved me and spent time with me, like I saw the dads in the neighborhood do with their kids.

My grandmother eventually could not withstand the beatings, so she had a nervous breakdown. Her condition did not improve as the days passed, but that did not dampen my grandfather's faith. I would ask him if she was going to get better and he would always reply, "God is in control!"

As a result of her nervous breakdown, she was given a nurse to help with her care during the daytime hours. When the nurse came, she would sometimes bring her daughter who was older than me. One day my grandmother had a doctor's appointment, so the nurse decided to leave her daughter there to babysit me because I was young and very active. While they were gone, the daughter lured me into the front bedroom and made me have sex with her. This happened on other occasions, continuing to corrupt my innocence. Because of my stepfather's name calling and the molestations by the nurse's daughter, I began to think this type of sexuality was normal.

As time progressed, my grandmother eventually lost all sense of what was going on around her. One night while I was playing, I remember hearing this voice saying, "Go check on your grandmother." When I found her, she was sitting on the kerosene heater while it was hot, thinking that it was her chamber pot. She was burned very severely. For two weeks she was in a coma. When I went to the hospital, she woke up out of her coma and said to me, "I love you Junior and I always will." Twenty minutes after we left the hospital, we were sitting in the living room of my grandfather's home and the phone rang. It was my uncle, asking my grandfather if he'd heard the news that my grandmother just passed away. I ran in the room, crying. My neighbor, who became like a mother to me, grabbed me, comforted me and told me that it was going to be okay. My world was spiraling downhill because the only person on this earth that truly loved me was now taken from me.

Two weeks after my grandmother passed away, the phone rang and I said, "Hello." A voice replied, "Hey baby." I asked, "Who is this?" The voice replied, "It's me, your grandmother. Don't you remember me?" It was my grandmother's voice, but it was a demon that was calling me on the phone. I slammed the phone down and ran to my grandfather and cried. *Can you imagine knowing someone is dead and hearing their voice on the telephone?* This was very tormenting and it was only the first encounter with my dead grandmother. On another occasion I was looking at a picture of my grandmother and me and the picture changed shapes. My grandmother's figure began to move, so I threw the picture down because demons had manifested through our picture. *For many people, encountering this level of demonic activity would have given them a first class ticket to the nearest psychiatric ward, but thanks be unto God, He kept me!*

For a long time I would not look at her picture nor answer the phone. I was severely afraid because I had no one to turn to and no one who would actually believe me. My grandfather would laugh and tell me to "go somewhere and sit down." Sadly, I could only talk to God, who I didn't even believe existed! Even though I was tormented by these demonic beings, my curiosity with spiritual things only grew. I even began to wear a symbol of (what I thought was) the devil around my neck. It was the common symbol of Satan with the red skin and black horns - the image that had been painted to me. I would tell others that Satan was all-powerful and he was greater than this God that others talked about. I can imagine God was waiting for the day that I would come to know him as God and as my Savior.

Was God with me at this point in my life? Yes. God promised that He would always be with us and guess what? He is with us during our ignorance also!

Around the time my grandmother died, there was a movie that came out that was so demonic the news anchors gave out warnings that parents should not allow their children to watch it. The movie was called *The Exorcist*. Again, my curiosity got the best of me even though I was afraid, and I watched the movie. After this, I would sit in dark rooms, trying to get my eyes to turn green like the little girl in *The Exorcist*. Night after night I sat, calling on demonic powers until it finally happened - my eyes looked as green as I saw in this movie. It scared me badly but this is what I had asked for night after night. I even started seeing a demon that looked just like the girl in *The Exorcist*. Her head would manifest on the walls and mirrors.

As time passed the presence of demons became more and more common to me and I felt I had power. I would try to levitate objects with my mind and try to open and close doors too. My grandfather would try and talk to me about what I was doing, but it only strengthened my resolve to stay on that course. I believed that I was possessed by demons because they would manifest through me, especially when my grandfather would try and talk to me. A demon enters a human body when we lay down our will to them and *guess what?* I'd happily laid down my will to them. One night in particular, these demons manifested through me and even though I was much smaller in size than my grandfather, I picked him up by the throat and threw him across the room. After it was over I felt so horrible, but I had no control over what had just happened. *What had I done?* I didn't know what to do.

Lessons from the Journey

Horror movies are very demonic and they are created by demonic influence. Only a demon can reveal some of the stuff that is being showed in the movie theaters year after year. I am a firm believer that the devil is trying to show people that he is just as real as God is, but magnify himself over God.

Life sometimes can throw some heavily-weighted tests at us from which, to be honest, it may appear that we may never recover. Faith looks adversity in the face and declares, "God is able!" Our faith will be challenged throughout our lifetime, but we have to understand that God is like a fitness trainer who is helping us develop our spiritual muscles. Sometimes when our spiritual muscles are being developed, we experience great pain. But those tears will heal AND we will be made stronger! In order for muscles to rebuild, it takes protein. How do we get that essential protein? Simple, it's all in the word of God. The word of God has high doses of protein that is more than suitable to rebuild our spiritual muscles after life's tests seem to tear us down. The Psalmist knew the potency of God's word as he declares in **Psalms 119:26-28 *"My soul clings to the dust; Revive me according to Your word. I have declared my ways, and You answered me; Teach me Your statutes. Make me understand the way of Your precepts; So shall I meditate on Your wonderful works. My soul melts from heaviness; Strengthen me according to Your word."***

CHAPTER THREE

Economic Hardship

> Psalm 41:1 "Blessed is he that considereth the poor: the LORD will deliver him in time of trouble."

As a result of my grandmother dying, we now lacked money, so I often went to school in hand-me-down clothes and the kids picked on me badly. We went without food for many days because my grandfather only had an income of $515.00 a month from his Social Security benefits. What he lacked in money, he made up in his faith in God.

He was a faithful deacon in his church, but more importantly, I saw the way he lived his life. He was a man of prayer and strong faith! As a child I had extremely bad nosebleeds that sometimes kept me from playing like the other kids. My grandfather, and mother when I visited her, would try things like hanging keys down my back, pinching my nose, or holding my head back with a cold rag. Finally, my grandfather laid hands on me, in the name of Jesus, and commanded the nose bleeds to stop. Surely they stopped! Now I could finally run, play hard, and not worry about the nosebleeds.

Often when we sat in the house, hungry, my grandfather would drop down on his knees and pray. On many occasions, before he could get up, someone would knock at the door and say, "Cousin Johnnie, I cooked all this extra food and I thought about you and Jr." The Lord answered his prayer and our need!

There were many days that I came home from school and the only food there would be from the Meals on Wheels program. My grandfather would go without eating just so I could eat. He was so generous; he would feed others when they came around, although we didn't have any food to spare.

Our house also did not have insulation, so in the winter it was extremely cold and in the summer it was extremely hot. We did not have hot water, so for baths we would heat up water on a hot plate during the summer months and use a kerosene heater during the winter. But my grandfather was a survivor who had great faith in God and we endured. I, on the other hand, was angry that we were so poor. As children, we often do not understand the struggles our parents go through to maintain a home and to provide for us.

Once, my grandfather saved all year long to buy an Atari video game for me as a Christmas gift. At the time, this was the game that everyone wanted and anyone of importance in the neighborhood owned one. About two weeks before Christmas, my grandfather, being such a kind- hearted person, gave this young man a ride from one side of town to the other. Unfortunately, this young man used his kindness as an opportunity to steal my grandfather's wallet. My grandfather came home, broken-hearted, and said, "Junior, someone stole my wallet with the money for your Atari." I cried because I'd told all my friends I was getting an Atari, so when Christmas rolled around, all of my friends were knocking at the door, wanting to play the game. I told many lies so I wouldn't look bad, but of course my friends figured it out and picked on me really badly. That Christmas, all I received was a new basketball and nets for my basketball goal. I was totally inconsolable and many Christmases followed when I got nothing at all because we were so poor.

To this day, I cannot enjoy Christmas fully because the painful memories of those many Christmas mornings often replay in my mind. God has blessed me with a wife who showers me with gifts and love, even though I am still wounded by my past. I thank God for her every day! She has loved me for who I am and never rejected me because of how I look or my mistakes. She has been the one to show me what having a family is like, and what *being* a family really means.

Lessons from the Journey

I faced so many hardships as a child. If you are facing hardships now, I am here to serve you notice that you are going to make it through this! There are going to be better days! When I was growing up, my stepfather would not help and made a lot of promises that he never kept. I am so glad that God my heavenly Father never made a promise that He would not keep. If God said that He is going to do something, He is going to do it. The bible says in ***Matthew 24:35, "Heaven and earth shall pass away, but my words shall not pass away."*** So, God stands behind His word and will fulfill His promises in your life, no matter what it looks like.

Sometimes, we can go through problems and feel as if we are the only ones experiencing the trauma, but what I have learned about God is that what He allows you to go through is for someone else. Yes! I said it, what you are going through will give you compassion for others. God allowed me to go through all that trouble just for you! Be encouraged, your trouble has an expiration date and you are almost there! The bible says in ***Galatians 6:9, "and let us not be weary in well doing: for in due season we shall reap if we faint not."*** Often when someone gives up, it is right at the door of his or her breakthrough! So many times we fail to realize that things become the hardest before they get better. If you are in a heated battle that is a clear sign that the end is near.

CHAPTER FOUR

Troubles at School

> *Psalm 13:1-2 "How long wilt thou forget me, O LORD? forever? how long wilt thou hide thy face from me? How long shall I take counsel in my soul, having sorrow in my heart daily? how long shall mine enemy be exalted over me?"*

I often told God that He made a mistake in creating me. I believed for so long that I was the scum of the earth and that my life was a mistake. How could my life be valuable if my own mother chose to give me away instead of raising me? It also hurt that I looked nothing like my sisters, and that was another avenue for kids to talk and pick on me. They would question if my father was white, Puerto Rican, or Mexican. My complexion separated me from my mother, sisters, the kids at school, and it separated me from the man whose name I bore. My stepfather voiced his hatred toward me every day and it hurt more than you could ever imagine. It tore down my confidence on every level. I desired to have a father that spent time with and told me how proud he was of me, but all I ever heard from my stepfather instead, was how worthless I was.

I went to school day after day and no one knew all the things that were going on with me. The kids would question why my clothes weren't as nice as theirs. They also picked on me because my clothes were sometimes dirty. We didn't have money to go to a laundromat, so my grandfather washed everything by hand in a bathtub with cold water. He would use an old washboard and scrub and scrub, but to be honest, my clothes looked just as dirty as before he got started. Even though I now know that my grandfather was doing the best he could, it was very difficult for me to endure being picked on. I could not understand why things were so bad for us. It was especially hard when I saw other kids who had nice clothes and their fathers around. To me they seemed to have it all.

The demon powers showed me how to control my body to the point that I could make myself run a fever or feign sickness in other ways. I missed so many days from school that a truancy officer came to my home to find out what was going on, but I didn't know how to tell anyone what I was going through. I prayed night after night, "God please take me from this," and I even thought of ways that I could kill myself. My prayer was that God would kill me because I felt that death was my way out, but I am so glad that God did not answer my prayers and looked over my ignorance.

As time went on I started hanging on the streets, trying to fit in with a rougher crowd. I thought if I could be like those boys, people would accept me and look past the difference in my complexion. Instead of total acceptance, the adults were talking about me. As the old saying goes, "I couldn't win for losing." The adults were saying, "It's a shame that your grandparents have raised you in church and now you want to hang on the block where all the drunks, crack addicts, weed heads, etc., are." My grandmother, on my mother's side, would tell me how much she hated me because I hung out on the streets. *Can you imagine getting so much hate from people who you thought truly loved you?* I was such an embarrassment to them. People didn't understand that I was just crying out for help, but no one was listening.

    I was better off with the people on the street. They were too caught up in their own issues to care about my complexion. I really thought I was finally fitting in. Day after day, as an eight-year old boy, I would walk up the block and hang around the pool halls, seeing people shoot pool, fight, and get drunk. I would also go to what we called in our town, 'the mini park', where everyone went to learn how to play basketball and just hang out. This is where I learned how to play, and gained my love for the sport of basketball. My dream was to one day go on to the NBA and be a professional basketball player like Magic Johnson, Larry Bird, or Kevin McHale, just to name a few.

    Besides basketball, I also learned how to play football and baseball. I could not have predicted that people would start accepting me because of my athleticism. I worked extra hard because I wanted the attention. Although I was getting attention on the field and court, once I went back home, it was back to torment, negative voices, and hard times. When we had games, I often wore hand-me-down shoes or shoes that had holes in them. This really didn't matter, but it still made me feel like an outcast. What's more, I was born with congenital cataracts; so as a result, I had to wear very thick glasses. This gave the kids something else to pick on me about, and even more ammunition for me to pray to God to take my life to get me away from all of this heartache. I eventually stopped wearing the glasses but I couldn't see well enough to keep playing baseball. Basketball became my sport of choice and football was a close second. I practiced extra hard to become the best. I had big dreams, but I lacked the confidence to really make my dreams become reality.

Even though my athleticism was gaining me respect, there was still a void in my heart and no one knew that I was so broken. I sought love from my mother and my sisters, but it seemed when I visited them that my mom and sisters didn't want me around either. Many times I would eat all their food and it would make them mad, but they did not understand I was just hungry from frequently going without food. Like my stepfather, my mother would often tell me that I would never be anything. *Wow! What a low blow.* One of my sisters even went on to say that she actually hated me. This was heart-breaking because she was the one sister that I loved very dearly! To this day we do not have a relationship.

I hated leaving my visits with my mom and sisters, even dealing with their disgust, because I had to return to a home where I was tormented by demons that were relentless in their attacks on my mind and body. At night I could see the dark shadows moving around the room and sometimes I could even hear and feel them whisper in my ears. As powerful as my grandfather was in prayer, it was no match for the powers of darkness that were trying to make me go insane. I thought I was going to lose my mind! At this point in my life I became very close to my next-door neighbor, Mrs. Mildred Slaughter. She was a remarkable woman and a godly mother-figure that I could always talk to when things were going wrong in my life. The devil also knew that I loved her like she was my mother. One night, while my grandfather and some of the members from the church were there, I was playing in the hallway, as usual. Mrs. Mildred walked in the back door, startling me! *Well, I thought it was her.* It was, in fact, a demon that disguised itself as Mrs. Mildred and when I saw what I thought was her, the demon called me to it. When I started walking towards her, something grabbed me. When "whatever it was" grabbed me, the demon then revealed itself. It turned to this ugly, black, enraged, demonic being that reopened the back door and walked out.

Lessons from the Journey

Constantly, day in and day out, I had to endure the brutal attacks of a stepfather who hated me because of the color of my skin. The mental anguish was often crippling and very degrading to my confidence. Many times my stepfather would get drunk and go on rants in front of people, where he would say things like, "I am not getting anything for that bastard. He is not my son." As a child I remember being so distraught and embarrassed that he would do this in front of people. I believed that I was white trash, even though I was living with black people. Yes, I am a biracial man and I have come to terms with that, but the rejection that I experienced pushed me so many days to want to commit suicide. Suicide, many times, seems to be the easy way out but it isn't. As long as there is breath in your body there is still hope and God has not given up on you yet!

I have often heard people say, "You are older now, so you should get over the fact that you don't have a father." I beg to differ! Unless you have gone through the pain of not knowing who your father is, it is hard to understand the depth of it! A father is the one who validates you as a man or woman, so often times if we do not allow God to fill and heal that void, we search for a father through various means. Sadly, I believed for many years that my stepfather was my real father because I was named after him. My mother perpetuated the lie for a long time. I have asked her, on several occasions, who my father is and she still refuses to tell me the truth. I often wondered why my mother would be so cruel, but when the devil is out to destroy you, it doesn't matter who he uses to do so.

If you are facing the same struggle, you have to learn the same lesson that I did: God is my father and I am not a mistake! Yes I said it! You are not a mistake! When God reveals who you really are and that your pain is a part of your purpose, it will help ease your heart and give you a heart of forgiveness! Not only forgive the people who have hurt you, but forgive yourself! God ordained your entrance although it may have and still may be rough, but I am here to tell you He has a great purpose for your life!

I want to leave this with you: God knows the thoughts that he thinks towards you, not Satan!

CHAPTER FIVE

The Rejected Dreamer

> *Genesis 50:20 "But as for you, ye thought evil against me; but God meant it unto good, to bring to pass, as it is this day, to save much people alive."*

After experiencing this last demonic event, I became more afraid. I couldn't tell anyone what I was going through because people would have thought that I was surely hallucinating or simply crazy. It was a lot like Joseph, when God began to show him, through night dreams, what he had promised concerning his life. According to Genesis 37:5, Joseph dreamed a dream and told it to his brethren and they hated him more than ever. His brothers already hated him because their father, Jacob, loved Joseph more than all his children. This was due to the fact that Joseph was the son of his old age, and Jacob made him a unique coat of many colors. His brothers saw the favor that was bestowed upon him and they hated him, as a matter of fact, they could not speak nicely to him.

I felt like Joseph. I was hated and picked on, even by my family. I felt unloved, neglected, rejected, and violated. Like Joseph, I loved my family but my family didn't love me because I wore the skin of a different color. People thought that my grandparents were spoiling me, but they actually weren't. They took care of me and offered me what they could, but between the poverty and the contempt from their son and my other relatives - I knew I was an unloved and unwanted child because of the way I looked.

God was revealing His plan in Joseph's life and out of sheer innocence he told it to his family and they laughed at him. According to Genesis 37:18, Joseph's brothers saw him coming afar and before he got close to them, they conspired to slay him. They mocked him and said to one another, "The dreamer is coming." Joseph's brothers not only devised a plan to slay him but they followed through with it. They threw him in a pit, essentially trying to stop God's will.

Like Joseph, the devil's plot for my life was to slay and cripple me with fear to the point I didn't believe in God or myself. There were times when I visited my mother's house, that my mother made my sisters put a dress on me. They thought it was cute, but it had an effect on my character. My stepfather didn't know about this, but once when we were arguing, he told me that my mother always thought I would turn out to be gay. She had three girls and I was the only boy, and she really wished I were a girl too. They had no idea what this had done to me. It opened the door even wider for a demon of lust to enter my body.

There were days that I would walk around the house naked and couldn't control myself. I would salivate and lay out on the floor and my grandfather would try to contain me, but could not. My life was seemingly just getting worse.

As the bible story progresses, Joseph's brothers not only threw him into the pit, but now they added another layer of hateful behavior by selling Joseph to a company of Ishmaelites. Joseph's brethren thought that they could kill the dream and promise on his life, but actually, they were getting him one step closer to his destined place. The price for Joseph's life was valued at 20 pieces of silver. (Genesis 37:25-28). The people in my life placed a low value on my life because they couldn't see what God saw, that God made me unique for a reason. I even hated looking at myself in the mirror because all I saw was a failure, a reject, and a demon-controlled and possessed young man. There were many times I would look in the mirror and these demons would manifest themselves through me and my face would be disfigured. I saw a young man that everyone hated. I saw a young man hated by his mother because he was a result of her whoredom! I hated my own self and my life. I would go to school and smile and it appeared I loved my life, but then go home at night and cry because I didn't fit in. The reality was my family hated me and people hated me and I couldn't understand what I had done that would make me an outcast and black sheep.

Lessons from the Journey

I just wanted to die. Life has a way, if you allow it, to silence you by throwing so much at you that you just give up. I can imagine Joseph felt the same way because these were the people that were supposed to have his back and love him unconditionally. Family is supposed to be there when there is no one else, but what do you do when even your family turns their backs on you? David was familiar with this feeling and he trusted that the Lord would take care of him. He expresses in **Psalms 27:10 "For my father and my mother have forsaken me, but the Lord will take me in."** I had to learn that God is all the family I need when everyone else turns their back on me.

Part II

CHAPTER SIX

Learning about Family

> *"So, amid the conflict whether great or small,*
> *Do not be disheartened, God is over all;*
> *Count your many blessings, angels will attend,*
> *Help and comfort give you to your journey's end."*[ii]

During the time I was heavily into sports, hip-hop hit the scene and it took the music industry by storm. I remember when break dancing emerged too and I loved it! I spent many days dancing on cardboard boxes, learning how to free-style, pop, windmill, and other dance moves. At the Ayden Collard Festival, a crowd was gathered, watching some guys breakdance in the foyer of the town hall. I felt like I was good enough to jump in and I did! My moves were tight and I got overwhelmed because I foolishly challenged three topnotch dancers. Out of nowhere this guy, whom I had never seen, jumped in and helped me battle the great dancers. Afterwards, I walked with the young man and his family to their car. Little did I know this encounter would be a life-changing experience! This family, the Gardners, would eventually accept me into their circle and love me just as if I was a blood relation!

Even though I loved sports, break dancing became a lot more important to me. Dancing allowed me to transcend my emotional and self-esteem issues. Dancing gave me hope because I was able to press past the negative chatter and no one could deny that I was one of the best in town. Instead of having to physically fight, I could do what we called on the street, *battle*[iii] someone, and win. I practiced hard to be the best, and I started getting recognition around town. Even though I gained a new level of respect and acceptance, I still had to go home to a drunken stepfather who cursed me and my grandfather out each time he was intoxicated or high on drugs. The family, who I'd met at the festival, invited me to dinner and to hang out with the young man who would become my best friend and big brother.

As I was talking to Mrs. Gardner, I told her who my grandmother was, and I was shocked that she knew her. It turned out they were my cousins. Look at how God had allowed our paths cross! God sent them into my life at the right time when things were really spiraling downhill. I had finally found a family that accepted me and loved me despite my appearance and shortcomings. My godmother, Juanita Gardner, who is an amazing woman, taught me how to receive love and that there was a better side of life. The Gardner family was a very loving family. Although they were not perfect, they had a genuine love for each other and me. I went to visit one weekend dressed in dirty clothes because it was all I had to wear. When Mrs. Gardner saw me, she gave me some of her son Ernie's clothing and washed everything I had on - underwear and all. This meant a lot to me because I know she probably thought, "Where did this dirty kid come from?" But the only thing she showed me was unconditional love.

In my regular life, my stepfather came home at 4pm, drunk, just getting off work, and broke because his so-called friends would get him drunk and take his money. One particular Friday evening I was having fun dancing and playing in front of my grandfather's house when a car drove up. Suddenly, the back door flew open and someone pushed my stepfather out of the back seat, right into the ditch. He was a drunken mess! Cursing and raising pure hell as he got up off the ground, he cursed me out and my grandfather too. He then went in the house and got a knife and threatened to stab my grandfather and me.

After that, he chased his girlfriend down the street with the same knife, actually trying to stab her. We all ran for our lives because we found out that he was not only drunk, but also high on heroin. Later that night he came back for round two. He was cursing and pushing my grandfather and me around; it got so bad that he and my grandfather got into a fistfight. *Can you imagine an 80-year old man fighting a 30-year old younger, stronger man? Yes, it went down.* My stepfather was wailing on my grandfather like he was a stranger off the street and not his father.

Finally, my grandfather mysteriously gained some strength and put a whipping on my stepfather that he hasn't recovered from to this day! *And my grandfather has been dead for over 20 years!* The situation, though, drove me deeper into bitterness and anger. I was fed up with this man who called himself my father and would bring himself to do such things. As a result, the devil had more frequent visits with me and showed me how I could take his life and mine too, in the process. Thankfully I didn't carry that plan out and instead I went to dancing to ease my mind. Even though I was playing sports, nothing calmed me like dancing.

Lessons from the Journey

It was amazing meeting my godmother and knowing what it was like to have a family that believed in me. I am here to tell someone, although I may not know you, I believe in you! Believe in yourself! God has invested so much in you and he expects a return on his investment. The bible says in **2 Corinthians 4:7 "but we have this treasure in earthen vessels, that the Excellency of the power may be of God, and not of us."** God wants to manifest his power through you! He has put something so great and powerful in you so that the devil fears your potential! Understand that the trouble you are facing can catapult you into your designed and divine purpose.

CHAPTER SEVEN

Struggling with School Work

> *1 Samuel 16:7 "For the LORD sees not as man sees: man looks on the outward appearance, but the LORD looks on the heart."*

By now I was in middle school and I was struggling. My fifth grade teacher had so much compassion for me that she convinced the school to hire a tutor to help with me with social studies and study skills classes. My tutor's name was Mrs. Carolyn Dunn. I remember her so distinctly because she was the only one who believed in me, besides my godmother and grandmother. She saw something in me and pulled it out. She gave me confidence in my own ability and taught me how to study effectively. I will never forget the impact Mrs. Dunn had on me and for the first time I felt like I was somebody special. I looked forward to our weekly visits and I remember crying when she told me that our meetings had to come to an end. The sessions were therapy to me because I was with someone who accepted me for who I was as a human being and because she did not look down on me because of my appearance.

I was finally able to keep up in class and turn in my homework without feeling ashamed or dumb! My fifth grade teacher, who looked past the hard kid and saw something worth salvaging, had gotten me help so I could thrive. I didn't realize how much she believed in me too. God was building a group of people in my circle that loved me unconditionally. This gave me so much momentum going into the next school year. I was able to study, do homework, and pass my tests with flying colors. Also, my weekly visits with my godmother were fulfilling because it gave me some sense of belonging.

While I was gaining confidence in one area, I still lacked it other areas. Back at school, the kids were still relentless with picking on me about my clothes. *Man, it seemed like I got out of the pot right into the frying pan!* I soon became frustrated with life again because all the momentum that I had gained was sapped right from me. I started faking sick, missing day after day, and getting further and further behind. The school called the truancy officer on me again to figure out why I was missing so much school. I was called into the office to talk with the truancy officer who wanted an explanation for why I was missing so many days. I lied, of course, because I was too ashamed to tell the gentleman that the kids were picking on me because I didn't have sufficient clothes.

My grandfather started telling me stories about heaven and how one day, if we serve God, we can go there and He would give us wings like angels. *Like angels?* I was rather curious, and I wanted to know more about God. I decided to pick up the bible and read the book of Revelation and man did I love it! I read it over and over again. Each time it seemed as if the words were jumping off the pages and becoming alive to me. It's not that I hadn't ever been to church, but I never paid attention while I was there and for the most part, I truly hated every time I went! To me, the pastors seemed like they were in a karate match while they were preaching. I started reading the bible more, especially the book of Revelation, because it talked about a lot that really caught my interest.

My interest in Jesus really heightened but the mental attacks from demonic spirits also increased. The thoughts of suicide were stronger because of the spiritual things happening and also because of the economic hardships. Many days I only ate the meal I received at school. I did not want to go home after practice because we didn't have food there and I knew that I would be tormented by black spirits.[iv] Thankfully, I had sports to distract me during eighth grade. Our football team was undefeated and I was the starting center, on offense, and one of the starting corner backs, on defense. In basketball, I was the leading scorer and I had finally become popular among the fellas and the girls.

This popularity led to my first relationship and I was on top of the world because a peer finally saw me as a person and not the dingy, dirty, dirt-dobbler I was being called. As a young man all I saw was bad examples of relationships, so, of course, I followed what I saw. Because of my inexperience and low self-esteem, the relationship didn't last long. I was extremely possessive, but looking back, it is not surprising considering I didn't know how to treat a woman or love healthily.

Lessons from the Journey

I was thankful for those times when people saw there was more to me than what was on the outside. As you see in my story, even in my moments of peace or normalcy, turmoil was waiting around the next corner. Often there are things in our lives that appear to be normal, but in actuality, the devil is working behind the scenes to set up traps to stop what God has predestined for our lives. I don't know who you are reading this text, but know that God has His hands on your life to do some great and wonderful things. You may be in a hard place right now, but I am here to serve you notice that God has sent angels to fight for you and to bring you through to a new and better place in your life. Don't lose heart nor faint in your mind because your best days are ahead of you.

CHAPTER EIGHT

Cycle of Addiction

> *Proverbs 31:6 – "Give strong drink unto him that is ready to perish, and wine unto those that be of heavy hearts."*

When school was out for the summer I started hanging out more on the streets, searching for validation. I remember one night in particular, a group of my older friends were drinking and offered me some alcohol. I declined, but one of them replied, "Either you drink it or you will wear it home." I thought if they poured it on me I couldn't cover up the smell of the liquor which was called Thunderbird, but if I drink it…well you know the rest. I went home feeling like I was now a part of something that would gain me some respect.

I had no idea that this would start a vicious cycle of alcohol addiction at the age of 13. I also didn't understand the rippling effects that would transfer over to every area of my life. The thing about Satan is that he will show you how great something can be but he will not show you all the heartache and pain that will be associated with a dumb decision. I was addicted to Thunderbird, which was a strong wine. I felt that I finally found my niche. I couldn't live without it now.

I remember one night I thought I would show off and I guzzled down two-fifths of Thunderbird. I was so drunk. That night I broke my grandfather's heart! He was so disappointed that I came in drunk, but what he didn't understand is that it was a learned behavior. It gave me the key to finally fit in and be named amongst those that were seemingly "somebody" in town. The next day I slept all day long and my grandfather waited patiently for me to awake. He fussed me out so bad and I hated that I let him down. Even though I disappointed him, I couldn't stop drinking. I became very clever with ways to fool my grandfather about my drinking, like coming in a little tipsy instead of totally drunk.

I wasted most of my summer drinking, so I missed football camp for Junior Varsity my first year of high school. My football coach was disappointed and I felt bad that I let someone else down that I really admired. I started drinking more and I added marijuana to my list of bad habits. I would go to school high and try to do my work, but I struggled terribly.

Finally, basketball season rolled around and I went out for tryouts and I made the team! Excited and ready to ball, I was able to move up to varsity for a couple of games because the starting point guard was still playing football. While I was gaining success in the area of basketball, my home life was still deteriorating fast. As a result, I moved in with my godmother for much of the basketball season.

I was so afraid playing on the varsity team! I messed up so bad at the beginning because of fear, but after the first couple of quarters I was able to get comfortable as the point guard. When I would come home to my godmother's house, it was nice to be able to eat a decent meal and not be constantly in the middle of turmoil.

Ninth grade was the worst year of my life. I started skipping class, going to school high and drinking more. I failed my grade and at that point I didn't care anymore. I felt like what my mom and stepfather said was true about me and that I was, in fact, a failure.

For the summer, I went to New Jersey and I landed my first job at McDonalds. I lied about my age to land the job, but I was finally able to work and make my own money. Sadly, my aunt's sons were straight alcoholics. Every Friday we would fill a giant cooler with a wide assortment of alcohol and we would drink straight through until Sunday evening. I left North Carolina weighing 153 pounds. When I returned, after being there for two months, I weighed over 230 pounds. I ate very well and drank copious amounts of liquor. It seemed all I accomplished that summer was gaining all that weight and becoming an even more skillful drinker.

I returned to North Carolina and no one recognized me. I was so overweight that I couldn't play basketball as skillfully as before. I was 15 years old and I had a terrible addiction. When I went back to school the following school year, people picked on me terribly because I was so heavy. I gave up basketball, and since that was all I cared about I wanted to drop out of school, but I couldn't because I wasn't old enough. I hated school more and more. As the year went on I started skipping class and staying home from school more frequently. Because I was in high school at that point, no one really cared - if they noticed.

My grandfather's health was failing and we still struggled badly just to eat, let alone pay the bills. We didn't have a working phone and we still couldn't afford to have gas in the tank to provide us with hot water. This meant I still went to school dirty sometimes, but because I was older, I was able to keep my clothes clean. The pressure that I was under was too much to bear.

Lessons from the Journey

Sometimes life can be like a whirlwind, and you can feel like you don't know which way is up. Life comes at you fast, the up and down roller coaster has no brakes, and you just want to give up! Since I have gotten older, I have come to understand that my life's course has been pre-orchestrated by God and He is fully aware of everything that I have faced and will face. The pain and disappointments were all a part of the equation and God is a good mathematician! In the book of ***Job 23:10,*** he declares: ***But he knoweth the way that I take: when he hath tried me, I shall come forth as gold.*** In order for God to get us to our predestined place in time, we must go through fiery places in life for God to, not only bring out what He has locked in our spirit, but to polish and make us into something that is shining with the glory of God. God's promises come with troubles attached to them and that is to help birth that promise into fruition. The bible declares: ***That I may*** *know him, and the power of his resurrection, and the fellowship of his sufferings, being made conformable unto his death; (Philippians 3:10).* We, as human beings, sometimes want what God has, but we do not want the sufferings that are attached to it. I have heard a great pastor say, "Can you stand to be blessed?" The blessing comes with struggles that are designed to birth your promise into fruition. Abraham went through great struggles to obtain the promises that God had given him, but according to the word of God, *"And so, after he had patiently endured, he obtained the promise."*

CHAPTER NINE

Unexpected Pressures

> *Psalm 38:17 "For I am ready to halt, and my sorrow is continually before me."*

When my tenth grade year was over and another long summer began, I started hanging out with known drug dealers for the popularity. As a result, I was always mistaken for one of the dealers, so the police harassed me all the time. Because this was happening, my mother sent me to live with her sister in New Haven, Connecticut for the summer.

I was not used to so much crime and the fast-paced life of the city. For example, there were constant shootings or often there would be stolen cars that would be stripped and left in my aunt's driveway. Even though life there was very different, that summer ended up being a defining time in my life. My aunt was very tough and she taught me responsibility and how to be a man. She taught me how to save my money and to spend wisely. I obtained a job for the summer at Popeye's, a fast food restaurant. I worked hard and I really enjoyed working with my family members who were employed there also. As the summer came to an end, seemingly very quickly, my plans were to live there permanently.

I called our neighbor down South, and asked him to bring my grandfather to the phone so I could speak to him. I became alarmed because my neighbor told me to come home because my grandfather was not doing well. Months before I had left North Carolina, I asked my stepfather, explicitly, to take my grandfather to the doctor regarding his foot. *If he had only had taken him, my grandfather would have never lost half of his right leg.* My grandfather had previously hurt his toe, but because a doctor never looked at it, he developed gangrene and it began to spread up his leg. The gangrene made his foot rot and it was very foul-smelling. Once I got word, I told my aunt that I had to move back to North Carolina to take care of my grandfather. She tried talking me out of it because she felt that I was too young to be taking care of an old man and would be missing out on life by doing so. My reply was, "He had taken care of me and the least I could do was to return the favor."

I caught a bus back home to North Carolina and my sister picked me up when I arrived. When I walked into the house, I could only cry because of the condition my grandfather was in! It was hard seeing my hero and the man I really viewed as my father in that shape. He was a devout, Christian man who was dedicated to serving as a deacon. He epitomized faithfulness because no matter how bad he felt, each week he was there like clockwork, making sure the church was clean and presentable. To see him in so much pain, and to think my no-good stepfather could have prevented this if he had only done what I asked him to do, was too much to bear. The next day after my return home, my next-door neighbor took us to the doctor's office to get his foot checked out and the report wasn't good at all. The doctor said that he needed to operate immediately so that he could stop the gangrene from spreading throughout his body. Of course, because he was in such bad shape, he could not sign any documentation for himself, nor could I sign for him because I was a minor. So I had to call my stepfather and threaten to kill him if he didn't do it. And because he knew that I was not that young child anymore who was afraid of him or that he could push around, he came and signed. The doctor was able to save from his right knee and above, and I was very grateful for that! It was very hard on my grandfather after that because he was a very independent man.

We were already struggling, but now the struggle became even worse. My grandfather was incapable of doing much because of his leg. It was hard seeing him go through so many days of frustration and pain, but we got through it. It caused me to mature very fast. I learned how to cook simple things very quickly so that we could survive. While this was going on I was becoming angrier and angrier because my stepfather had abandoned us! He would ride right past the house and never stop by to check on his father or me. I felt alone many nights knowing that we did not have sufficient food, clothing, water, or other basic necessities to survive. It was tough because I was going to high school again and worried about my grandfather's well-being. Later that year I went to the local

Burger King and got a job. I was working and making some money and boy was I happy! I was sixteen and I was at the age that I was able to drop out of school if I desired.

Lessons from the Journey

It was difficult having to grow up fast! When there is a great promise on your life, the devil will do anything and by any means necessary to stop you from reaching your purpose. I have learned that the greater the purpose, the greater the trials and difficulties. I can imagine David learned that lesson well as he was shivering in caves, wondering how he would one day wear a crown. Often times we have to go through these hard places to get where we are predestined to be in life. In 1 Samuel 22, even though David was hiding from Saul, those who were in distress and discontented were going out to be led by him! Even though he was far from being the official king, he couldn't help but begin to walk out what God had already ordained for Him.

Sometimes because we experience great trouble in our hurt, we feel that is how life is supposed to be. The truth is that all things are working together for God's glory! His plan is coming together.

CHAPTER TEN

Rock Bottom

Psalm 69:5 "O God, thou knowest my foolishness; and my sins are not hid from thee."

In school I was doing badly in my classes because I really didn't care any longer. I started hanging out with a bunch of guys who walked the streets aimlessly all day long, drank alcohol continuously, and were high school drop outs. This, to me at the time, seemed like the perfect life! *How foolish could I be to drop out of school and just hang out all day, every day, doing nothing with my life?* At this point, one of my cousins from New Jersey got wind of me dropping out of school and tried to get me to go live with her in Kinston, NC. I stayed for a couple weeks with her, but the streets were calling me. I went back home and started hanging on the streets again. It got bad because at night I would go without sleep and stay on the streets. One night, in particular, I had an epiphany. I woke up on someone's floor after getting drunk with all the guys and I looked around at all of them. They were drunk too! I remember thinking to myself, "I can do better than this!" I got up and went home in the wee hours of the morning.

 Here is the crazy thing, I had not been to school in about two months, but I decided to go back. People teased me so bad, but I really didn't care! I went to the front office and talked with the administrators, Mrs. Deborah Rogers and Mrs. Stella Vance, about what I needed to do. God gave me so much favor with them and they went to bat for me. They worked it out with the school and got me enlisted in summer school. I flew through summer school. It's not that I wasn't smart; I was just stupid in my decision-making. We all, at some point in our lives, make some decisions that we look back on and ask ourselves, "Did I really do that?" Sitting, writing this, I ask myself not only did I do that, but also, *how did I make it through that?*

 All during my eleventh and twelfth grade years I worked at Burger King, went to school, and took care of my grandfather. Even though I settled in my mind that I was going to finish school, I had a lot of difficulties at home. My grandfather was developing Alzheimer's, so I missed a lot of days of school due to that. One morning, while I was in class, Mrs. Rogers called me down to the office and while walking down I remember wondering what I had done? She called me to ask if everything was all right. "Alright, what do you mean?" I asked. She went on to explain to me that she and her husband had a police scanner at home. The night before, they heard a call for the police to go to my home. I was puzzled because I had to work that night so I got in late. When I got home that evening I asked my grandfather why the police was called and he denied it at first. But I persisted and he finally came out with it. He called the police because he thought that a man and two women came down from the ceiling and tried to rob him.

This was just one of the many things that he started doing as a result of developing Alzheimer's. He would use the bathroom on himself often and I had to leave school to deal with those issues. On another occasion he almost burned down the house. I came home one day and he had fried some chicken and poured the hot grease down the drain. Day after day I had to go to school, work, take care of him, and try to be a teenager. One good thing was at least I was able to buy some decent clothes so that no one picked on me about that any longer.

I reached out to my stepfather on several occasions to get some help from him with my grandfather, but he refused. One day my grandfather was very sick and needed to go to the doctor badly, but I had to work because we needed the money. When I finally got off work, I saw my stepfather sitting over at Super Dollar, so I went over there to talk to him. He would not roll down his window but I said what I needed to say, standing at the window. I told him that if he did not take my grandfather to the doctor and get him back home, that I was going to whip his behind! It worked! He not only took him, but he made sure that he got back home safely.

Lessons from the Journey

Many times we get to a hard, destitute place in life and cannot see what God is doing. You have to keep in mind that it's in your darkest place where God is preparing you for His use. When David was fighting for the Philistines, planning defense and escape routes, or leading his own disenchanted men, all those things were preparing him to be a better tactician and commander. Diamonds go through a deep dark process within the earth, but the process is creating something beautiful. The process to greatness is always tough, but my theory is this; whenever God gives a promise, he always gives a problem to birth that promise into fruition. It always gets the toughest before the promise is birthed.

Part III

CHAPTER ELEVEN

Trouble with Women

> *Psalm 27:5 "For in the time of trouble he shall hide me in his pavilion: in the secret of his tabernacle shall he hide me; he shall set me up upon a rock."*

I met this young lady who I thought was the perfect match for me. Because of my insecurities, it did not take long before I became serious. I became very possessive and thought she would be 'the one', but my grandfather warned me there was something about her he didn't like. He would say he just couldn't put his finger on it. I was young and a hot-head so I refused to listen to his warnings. She became my reason to go to school, but who would know that this would go south pretty fast? It turned out he was right; because of her, I would almost lose my life.

My mother lived across the yard from her family, but we hid the truth from her mom, fearing that she would stop our relationship. Sadly, we didn't have to! One of my sisters, the one who hated me, told her everything. As a result, her mother kicked her out and she went and stayed with her aunt for a while. My cousin took me to see her one night and when I walked up, there were some guys standing outside her aunt's door. I thought I was really tough so I walked up on them with my hoodie on and said, "What's up?" After I spoke, I turned my back and proceeded to walk into the house, not even noticing that they had pulled out guns. My cousin saw what was going on and blew his horn to draw their attention towards him and away from me. When I got fully in the house, the young lady told me that they had guns and that I should run out the back door.

I ran out the back door and headed to a close-by store and she went out the front door where my cousin faced the guys. My cousin bluffed that he had guns too, which seemed to be working. Like an idiot, she ran out and yelled my exact location to my cousin. *So guess what?* The guys heard her too. My cousin went left and they went right, racing to see who could get to me first, and unfortunately, the guys reached me first. In the meanwhile, I called her from a payphone and said, "Lock the door and call the police." While I was talking, I heard a car speeding into the parking lot and when I turned around, these guys jumped out their car and yelled, "Hey nigga." They started firing shots at me, so I dropped the phone and started to run. Out of nowhere, my cousin drove up from behind the store and told me to jump in. I remember seeing the bullets sparking on the ground and I could hear others flying past my head.

My cousin, Ernie drove up just in the nick of time because the bullet that was meant for my head hit the front end of the car. Once I'd jumped in, there was one guy close enough to grab me, but he chose to fire his gun instead. The bullets seemingly went right around the car. I didn't know then but I fully understand now, that I am older, that God had angels surrounding me. We were able to get out of the parking lot and the chase was on. We ran every stoplight, went down every one way street the wrong way, and exceeded speed limits, reaching over 100mph to try and get the police to pull us over. As usual, there were no police in sight when you need them, but God was with us. My cousin never eased off the gas pedal until we reached his house about 7 miles away in Grifton.

Only God could have kept us through all of that turmoil. Once we arrived in Grifton, the car died right in the front yard because the radiator was shot by the bullet meant for my head. The hole in the radiator was so big; it was a miracle that the car did not die on the highway while we were running for our lives. I had to go into hiding for a couple of months because I didn't know if they would come after me to finish what was started. My grandfather warned me many times that this girl was trouble, but because I was young and big-headed, I thought I knew better. It turned out she was messing around with one of those guys and she set me up! I was so angry and hurt, but like a fool I believed her lies. Even after that crazy scenario I couldn't leave her alone and kept pursuing her. Later that year, I thought everything was fine until I saw her walking down the hallway of the school with another guy. Again the words of my grandfather rang in my ears.

Lessons from the Journey

I grew up seeing my mother being physically and verbally abused by men and often seeing my stepfather abuse women. I found myself being attracted to young ladies who had come from similar backgrounds. When we are attracted to people who have gone through similar traumas, hurts and disappointments, it proves to be disastrous in the long run. Sometimes God will allow life's circumstance to get our attention. Just think about it. If it had not been for some trouble coming into our lives we wouldn't give God the time of day. In **Psalm 119:71**, the writer said, **"It is good for me that I have been afflicted; that I might learn thy statutes."** Trouble is not always a bad thing because some tests come to reveal who we are and show us the greatness of God. God sometimes hides Himself in our trouble so that we can seek after Him and get to know Him. We have often heard the story about the three Hebrew boys and how Nebuchadnezzar threw them in the fire to burn them up. In actuality, he was throwing them right where God wanted them to be so that people could see His glory. If you are in a heated trial right now, you are right where God wants you to be. What killed others will be the staging place for the King of kings and the Lord of lords to show Himself strong.

CHAPTER TWELVE

A New Season

> *Psalm 61:2 "when my heart is overwhelmed: lead me to the rock that is higher than I."*

As time went on my girlfriend and I eventually rekindled our relationship and she became pregnant. I was very scared because I was about to graduate and I had no idea how I was going to take care of a baby! While I was dealing with this, my grandfather's condition was getting worse. I was also on the borderline of failing my senior year of high school. Pressure was coming on every side and I felt like I couldn't handle it!

My principal had a meeting with all the seniors who were border-line failing because of attendance issues. I explained to him that I was missing so many days because my grandfather was sick all the time. I had missed beyond the limit, which was 21 days. He had mercy on me and excused 6 of my days which cleared my attendance just enough so I was still eligible to graduate. I felt good that I was graduating from high school, but at the same I was scared because I was about to enter into manhood. My anxiety grew the closer it got to graduation because I believed I was destined to be the failure my family expected me to become. A couple of weeks before school ended, Mr. Delano Wilson pulled me aside and said, "Frog, let me talk to you." I remember thinking, *what had I done?* He said to me, "Do you know you have a gift to teach?" *Me?* I thought this man had missed it because my mother told me that I was never going to be anything!

He had confidence in me and it caught me off guard because I was not the smartest kid in the class and I missed so many days from school that I could barely keep up with the school work. I went home wondering, *"Could I possibly do this?"* I then laughed because all I could hear were the dreadful words of scorn and mockery from my family. I thought the military would be a way out for me, but they would not allow me in because I was born with congenital cataracts. I couldn't see any other viable options. I thought about college but I felt that I would fail.

Soon after I graduated, my grandfather's condition worsened. Someone reported our living conditions to Social Services and they came out several times to inquire about the situation. Finally, social services made the decision that I was incapable of providing care to my 91-year old grandfather because the Alzheimer's had worsened and he was doing too many dangerous things. When the social worker told me that they decided to place him in a nursing home, I became very upset. I threatened her and she ran for her life. Later that day she came back with a Sheriff Deputy to remove him. I was powerless to stop them, and I had to face the fact that my crazy behavior wouldn't change anything.

What was I going to do? This man had been my rock, my dad, my everything! They took him to a nursing home in an area we call Little Washington. Even though that was a long drive to me, I would go and visit him once a week. While this was going on, my son was born and I was extremely distressed because I did not know how to be a father. I remember holding my son for the first time and thinking, "How am I going to do this?" *I brought a child in the world and didn't even know how I was going to take care of myself, let alone another life.* I always saw myself settling down and I believed that I should settle down and take care of the family I had seemingly created. I was still working at Burger King at night. It wasn't enough to support a family, but for the time being it kept money in my pocket.

When my grandfather was taken away, I dreaded the thought that I would have to stay with my mother. But I had to move in with her because I didn't know how to survive on my own and I didn't make enough money to be independent. She allowed me to stay with her and we bumped heads most of the time. She resented me because I looked like my father. When I brought my son to meet her for the first time, she only held him for about five minutes and gave him right back. His complexion was also fair, so I guess he was another reminder of her treacherous past.

Lessons from the Journey

According to 1 Corinthians 1:27-30 "But God hath chosen the foolish things of the world to confound the wise; and God hath chosen the weak things of the world to confound the things, which are mighty; And base things of the world, and things which are despised, hath God chosen, yea, and things which are not, to bring to nought things that are: That no flesh should glory in his presence. But of him are ye in Christ Jesus, who of God is made unto us wisdom, and righteousness, and sanctification, and redemption: That, according as it is written, He that glorieth, let him glory in the Lord." God had a plan for my life even though I could not see it at the time. To my family and others I was going to be a bum, but God saw me as more than a conqueror and a vessel that would one day bring him honor. He saw my end from the beginning. God saw me as the finished product but all people could see was a ruddy, little kid who didn't know his identity in Christ! Many people are going through life believing the negativity and doubt that people speak over their lives and never aspire to reach their dreams and goals. It has taken me years to fight through the negative words and the negative view that I had of myself. According to **Jeremiah 29:11 *"For I know the thoughts that I think toward you, saith the Lord, thoughts of peace, and not of evil, to give you an expected end."*** God knows the plans and thoughts that he has for your life despite the trouble and trauma you may be facing right now. I don't care how old you are, you can accomplish your dreams and goals!

CHAPTER THIRTEEN

The Soft Tugging

> *"Many times Satan whispers,*
> *"There is no need to try;*
> *For there's no end of sorrow,*
> *There's no hope by and by";*
> *But I know Thou art with me,*
> *And tomorrow I'll rise;*
> *Where the storms never darken the skies."*[v]

Around the same time, God sent one of my closest friends back into my life. He had become a Christian and began to talk to me about the Lord. Another friend, who'd become a minister, came along with him. I resisted. I felt like God didn't love me and that He couldn't save a person like me. Even though I struggled with God's love, my friends convinced me to start attending church. I remember going to a particular church and this lady stood up to testify, but right in the middle of her testimony she pointed to me and yelled, "God wants you!" She had an angry look on her face and, to be honest, I was a street kid so I got ready to punch the lady in response to her aggressive posture.

After initially just yelling and pointing, she was literally throwing chairs out of the way to get to me. I was scared, but it was not terror, it was a godly fear because I knew that God was in this lady and He was trying to get my attention. She finally reached me and got right in my face and said, "God wants you and there is a great call on your life!" I remember feeling the presence of God and I began to weep. He was touching this little, broken man that only knew hurt, pain, and rejection in his life. I still couldn't fathom that God accepted me and loved me for who I was, despite my flaws. *How could I receive love from anyone and especially a God who I didn't know and had never seen?*

God was dealing with me and the devil knew it too. My girlfriend wanted more of my time but I desired to go to church. Demonic visitations were happening more frequently, especially after that church service. There were nights that my bed would just shake and I would have demonic dreams that left me deathly afraid. Also, I experienced a series of troubling things that happened with my car.

One night after I left for work, something said to me, "Turn around." I wondered, *"Who just said that?"* because I'd never heard that voice before. Once I arrived at a stop sign, I heard the voice repeat the same thing. The voice became so loud that I had to obey! I drove past the stop sign and made a wide turn to go back home and all of a sudden my car's front end started shaking. I tried to make it home but the entire front of the car came apart and the front tires fell off and rolled down the street. I was terrified. What if I had sped around a curve at 55mph? I would have surely died that evening.

There was another incident on a night I drove my mother's car to work. I was coming out of Grifton, merging onto the highway and there was an 18-wheeler truck passing by at the same time. As I changed into the passing lane to pass the truck, the driver didn't see me and tried to move over. As a result I had to slam on the brakes to keep from going under the truck at 55mph. I slid over 100 feet out of control and remember thinking that I was going to die, but even in the midst of this, God sent an angel to protect me. The angel took the steering wheel from me and guided me safely into a ditch.

Some people from a nearby store ran down to the car to see if I was alright. One of the gentlemen who saw the accident wondered how I was able to keep control of the car. He said the way my car left the road, there was no reason that I should be standing there because the car should have flipped over, causing me harm. I was scared and shaking, but I didn't have a scratch on my body. I ran down to the store and called my mother to let her know what happened. When I dialed her phone number from a pay phone I had this gut-wrenching feeling that she was going to flip out and she did! My mother cursed me out for a good five minutes and to top it all off, she never asked if I was okay. Sadly, her car meant more to her than my life.

My mother and her friend pulled the car out of the ditch and there was not one scratch on it. The only thing out of the ordinary was some mud from the ditch that got on the bumper. The men who saw the accident told my mother that if anything different had taken place I would have died and that only God could have kept the car from flipping over. I went to work that night thinking that God was trying to send me a message. Having incidents with my car for several days in a row was starting to really weigh on my mind.

Lessons from the Journey

The road to what God has promised us can be very rocky and sometimes a little overwhelming. ***Psalm 61:2*** states, ***"From the end of the earth will I cry unto thee, when my heart is overwhelmed: lead me to the rock that is higher than I."*** It can get really tough and we have to turn to God for guidance because hard places in life can lead you in the wrong direction. Trials and tests can get us out of the seat of faith and into the back seat of a place called feelings. The bible clearly says in ***2 Corinthians 5:7 "For we walk by faith, not by sight,"*** so regardless of how it looks to our natural eye, we have to trust God! Sometimes God will allow some things to come your way that will make it appear that you have missed your purpose or He has forgotten about you, but I am here to tell someone who is reading this that you are right where God wants you to be! The bible tells how Jesus was led of the Spirit into the wilderness to be tempted of the devil, but even in the midst of one of his toughest hours, God was with him! So wherever you are right now in life, God is with you. During the process of walking into your promised place it can get really hard and really dark, but you have to remember that God promised He would never leave you in ***Matthew 28:20 "Lo, I am with you always."***

CHAPTER FOURTEEN

An Encounter with the Savior

> Matthew 11:28-30 *"Come unto me, all ye that labour and are heavy laden, and I will give you rest. Take my yoke upon you, and learn of me; for I am meek and lowly in heart: and ye shall find rest unto your souls. For my yoke is easy, and my burden is light."*

The next night, instead of going into work early, I went to the house of a friend who had been talking with me about the Lord. I walked into his house and said, "I am here to give my life to the Lord." He looked at me and said, "If you are not serious don't waste my time." When I convinced him that I was serious, we went to see my best friend so that he could lead me to the Lord. While we were driving to his house, every thought came to my mind why I shouldn't do it. At one point, I was tempted to keep driving past his house, but I didn't listen to those contrary thoughts. God was drawing me to Himself. Jesus says in **John 6:44, "No man can come to me, except the Father which hath sent me draw him: and I will raise him up at** *the last day."* That night I accepted Christ into my heart and I felt God change my heart. According to **2 Corinthians 5:17, "Therefore if any man be in Christ, he is a new creature: old things are passed away; behold, all things are become new."** For the first time in my life I was alive! My spirit was born again and I was birthed into a royal family. God had forgiven me and washed my sins away by the shed blood of Jesus that is powerful enough to cleanse away the sin of the whole world. We were born into sin, not because of anything that we have done, but as a direct result of Adam's disobedience in the garden. The writer of **Psalm 51 stated, "Behold, I was shaped in iniquity; and in sin did my mother conceive me."** No matter how good we are and how much good we do for people, it will never be good enough because Adam caused sin to be passed onto all of us.

I went to work late that night but when I got there my coworkers said to me, "There is something different about you." I was a little ashamed to tell them what had just happened to me, but the joy of the Lord was bubbling up on the inside of me. Life seemed to be different and everything looked to be brand new.

While this landmark event happened, there was still trouble brewing elsewhere in my life. I still faced the issue of my battle with demons. One night after my conversion I was given a cassette tape of a pastor preaching on the power of the blood of Jesus. I was listening to the sermon while at work when I saw two demons walk in the restaurant. I was there by myself so I was kind of scared. The two demons walked through the door that led to the kitchen and as I was looking at them with the sermon playing, I began to plead, "The blood of Jesus, the blood of Jesus," over and over again. I was merely repeating what I heard the pastor saying on the tape. After a few moments I stopped and I thought everything was okay, but as I was walking towards the sink, one of the demons threw a tomato slicer at me. I started pleading the blood really loudly. Other things started to fall but I continued to plead the blood of Jesus and, finally, I saw the two demons open the kitchen door and leave. This encounter with the demons was so real and definitive; it made me think about my life. I was in a toxic relationship that would definitely be in conflict with my new relationship with God. Also, my son was getting a little older and my job at Burger King wasn't enough to guarantee a secure future for him.

    I looked for a new job and that search led me to be hired as a helper at a construction site. I took pride in what I was doing, although we did the dirty jobs. I was able to quit Burger King because I was making *real* money. On the construction site there were many men that were supposed to be Christians but often times their character didn't match up with what they were preaching. Thankfully, I made many friends and newfound brothers in Christ elsewhere. I was finally able to leave my mother's house and all the negativity that was there.

    I moved in with one of my brothers in Christ because he wanted to help me get delivered from the sexual sin that was a stronghold in my life. One night I went to sleep and woke up in a very dark valley. I heard **Psalm 23:4** in my dream, as clear as day. I walked through this valley feeling scared, but all I kept hearing was **Psalm 23:4**

"Yea, though I walk through the valley of the shadow of death, I will fear no evil; for Thou art with me; Thy rod and Thy staff, they comfort me." I was walking around – although asleep, about to walk out the front door, when the other brothers heard and saw me and got up and began to pray. The brothers were in spiritual warfare for me because death was trying to take me. Demons kept showing up night after night and I decided it was best that I move back home to my mother's house. It was a hard decision but I did not want this part of my life to be a burden on anyone else. The brother that I was living with agreed because he was not used to demons on that level.

Also, even though I loved the Lord, I had some serious struggles from childhood that were hard to break. It's not that God wasn't able to free me, but this was something I had to want to let go. One day I had stopped by one of the ministers' house and talked with him about what I was dealing with and asked him to pray for me. He called some of the other ministers over to assist him in praying for me. Once the others arrived, they began to pray for me and I lost all control over myself. I was possessed by demons. It took about five preachers to hold me down while one of them cast the devils out of me. I was told that I was throwing up green liquid and saying things that I have no recollection of, to this day.

I received the gift of the Holy Ghost that day! I was free finally from the influence of the demonic spirits that had taken their abode in my spirit. After this, I moved back home only to lose my job and my car. It got really rough for a while. I not only lost my job, but I lost my car. There were many days that all I had to eat was the word of God! Some days, my mother would come home and sit in her car and eat, knowing that I had nothing to eat. I fasted and prayed, and read the word day in and day out. The word of God became meat for my soul. I would have to catch a ride to church and many nights I left there frustrated and desiring my old life style. There were nights that I got down to pray and I would fall asleep on my knees in the presence of the Lord. Oh, those were the days when God would allow me to feel His presence so strongly.

Even though I was growing spiritually strong, I would oftentimes go to sleep and be awakened by demons in my room. One night I went to sleep and I had an all-out fight with a demon and it finally got the best of me and grabbed me by the neck and started choking me. Then God came in my dreams, through the form of my former pastor, and killed this very strong demon. That morning, when I awoke from sleep, my sister said, "What happened to your neck?" The demon had actually been in the room and left a long scratch on my neck where it choked me. I became afraid because it wasn't just a dream. This demon had actually been in my room that night to try and kill me.

The visitations from the demons were relentless with the physical fights getting tougher every time. I woke up one night, standing on my bed, with my guard up from where I had been battling all night long. Some nights I would stand outside all night long because I was so tired of fighting demons. *Who could I tell and who would actually believe me?* Once, I was given some anointing oil during a church service and that night I went home and spread it around the house. I went to sleep afterwards, thinking everything was going to be fine, but while I was sleeping a demon began to whisper in my ear. I felt the demon's breath in my ear and immediately knew that it was in the room with me. I awoke out of my sleep and began to pray and the Holy Ghost began to pray through me. It was the first time in my walk with God that I had experienced spiritual warfare. For almost three hours I prayed and I felt the presence of some really strong demon powers. My mother came in that next morning and stepped in an oil spot on the floor and slid. I was so embarrassed and man did she put a piece of cursing on me that morning! After that fight with the demonic powers, I became even more fearful. I was ashamed to talk with anyone about what I was dealing with because I believed people would think I was crazy.

While I had given my life to the Lord and began to flourish in God's kingdom, I still had previous life issues to handle. I had only been saved for about six months and my girlfriend, at that time, allowed Satan to speak through her one day. God allowed me to hear the demon's voice and the demon said to me, "I am supposed to come before your God." I thought, "What? Really?" I remember laughing because I had just read about the time Jesus rebuked Satan when he spoke through Peter and tried to tell Jesus that He was not going to die and be raised again the third day. According to **Matthew 16:21-23, *"From that time forth began Jesus to shew unto his disciples, how that he must go unto Jerusalem, and suffer many things of the elders and chief priests and scribes, and be killed, and be raised again the third day. Then Peter took him, and began to rebuke him, saying, be it far from thee, Lord: this*** *shall not be unto thee. But he turned, and said unto Peter, Get thee behind me, Satan: thou art an offence unto me: for thou savourest not the things that be of God, but those that be of men."* You can plainly see Satan talks through anyone who yields himself, and in this case, Jesus dealt directly with the devil speaking through Peter. When I heard my girlfriend utter her demonic words, I was blown away because no one can come before God!

Now that I had given my life to the Lord, He would visit me in dreams and visions. One night, while I was sleeping, the Lord took me out into a night vision and showed some deceitful behavior my girlfriend was preparing to do. Guess what? Exactly as He showed me, it happened. I was hurt, but God had already told me through many prophets and my pastors that I was in an unhealthy relationship. My feelings were hurt but my pastor told me that it was just my flesh and for me to get over it!

Lessons from the Journey

I remember when I first received Christ into my life, it was the best but yet the toughest decision I had ever made. It was good in the sense because Jesus had come into my heart and flooded my soul with joy of His salvation. However, it was tough because I was deep in sin and to be honest I didn't want to let go of my past so quickly. The bible describes the struggle in **Hebrews 11:25** *"Choosing rather to suffer affliction with the people of God, than to enjoy the pleasure of sin for a season."* Sin has a pleasure that is undeniable and a grip that is hard to shack free from. It takes a made up mind and the raw power of God to set a man or woman free from its heinous clutches.

When you are called and predestined to do a work for the Lord Jesus Christ, all hell will be unleashed against your destiny. Look again at David; it was spoken to him in ***2 Samuel 7*** that his Seed would rule on the throne of Israel forever. In order for there to be an eternal ruler, there has to be an immortal who is also from David's mortal line. That could only be the God-Man, Jesus! God the Father had the plan of salvation, through David's line, set from eternity past, but Satan did everything He could to thwart God's covenant to David.

We could look at everything that happened between David's rule and Christ's birth, but let's just look at after He was born. Satan used Herod to murder all the male babies around Bethlehem ***(Matthew 2:16).*** That didn't work. When Jesus was mature, Satan tempted Him when he was weakened in the desert Bethlehem ***(Matthew 4:1-11).*** Satan then used Peter to try and rebuke Jesus for talking about His impending death ***(Matthew 16:22-23)***. And finally Satan's greatest failure at the cross! Satan did everything he could to stop God's plan, but God's covenant to David would be established 900 years after David's reign. We can be assured that ***"he which hath begun a good work in you will perform it until the day of Jesus Christ" (Philippians 1:6)!***

CHAPTER FIFTEEN

Losing My Grandfather

> "We must cease striving and trust God to provide what He thinks is best and in whatever time He chooses to make it available. But this kind of trusting doesn't come naturally. It's a spiritual crisis of the will in which we must choose to exercise faith."

While I was dealing with my heartache, my grandfather was at the point of death. I went to the nursing home to visit him and he was suffering badly. I said to him, "Daddy, go home and be with the Lord. I am grown now." I also told him I had given my life to the Lord and He will take care of me. He cried and so did I, but I knew that he would be better off in the arms of Jesus and not suffering any longer.

While my grandfather was on his deathbed, I got word that my grandfather hadn't paid the taxes on the house where we lived. I contacted my stepfather to let him know the situation. I hoped that he could get money to pay the taxes so that we wouldn't lose the house. While my stepfather was trying to raise the money to save his father's house, my mother heard about the tax situation. Instead of helping him, she devised a plan to trick my grandfather into signing over the house to her. She paid the taxes and obtained the deed of trust. She then went to the nursing home and carried out her plan.

I heard that she was going to do this and I tried to beat her to the nursing home, but I was twenty minutes too late! When I arrived, my grandfather said, "You just missed your mother." I asked him if, in his weakened state, he signed any papers. He said, "Yes." When I asked what he signed, he responded, "I signed papers to have the house fixed up for you to have somewhere to live." I explained to him that he had actually signed over the deed of trust to my mother. My grandfather was so hurt and disappointed by her deception, but he said, "Jr., if I had known what I was doing I would have rather had the town take the house than for your mother to have it." He told me to hurry up and stop her before she got to my cousin, Ella Hardy's house with the same lie. I left the nursing home, hoping I could get there before my mother, but I was unsuccessful. My mother ran the same scam on my elderly cousin. She then got a crew of people together to help her go in the house and throw out all of our belongings on the trash pile.

About two weeks after this incident, my grandfather finally went on to be with the Lord. I looked through my grandfather's insurance policies which he originally purchased for 25¢. The monetary value on them had increased to $250 at the time of his death. We were in a bad spot because we had no money to bury him. *What was*

I supposed to do, I was just a teenager? I turned to my stepfather, but he did not have any money to bury his own father. We all met at Mr. Norcott's funeral home to try and figure out what to do, not knowing my mother was going to show up too. Even with my grandfather's social security benefits, we still didn't have enough.

Mr. Norcott was a very kind man and my grandfather had done a lot of work for him through the years, so he decided to give us a generous discount. Even with that, we were short and had to find a way to fund the rest. I asked my mother if she would use my grandfather's house as collateral until we were able to pay the debt off. She nastily told us, "No!" She had already tricked my grandfather out of the house and I felt the least she could do was help! I lost it. *I could have killed her!* I had to be escorted out and one of the ministers from my church took me there to have my pastors pray for me because I was so hurt and angry. After my co-pastor prayed for me, I was able to forgive and go back and deal with the issue.

Even in the midst of this bad situation, God showed Himself strong. Someone agreed to pay the difference of $1200 so that my grandfather could receive a decent burial. The day of the funeral I had so many thoughts racing through my head. I was grieving the loss of one of the few people that ever loved me and I was hurt that only a handful of people came out to pay their respects to a man who had dedicated his life to helping others. *Wow!* All the folks that called him "brother" or "Deacon Johnnie" didn't even show up. While looking around and digesting all of this, I had to ask God to help me to forgive.

After the stress of the funeral and the burial was over, the reality set in that my grandfather was gone. I would never hear his voice again, telling me the right things at the right times that would always give me hope. Without his presence, it made it even harder to think about moving back into his house – now my mother's house. She began to fix it up so we could live there; not realizing it was a place of torment for me. I had experienced so many hardships there and the thought of moving back was a deep, grudging feeling that I could not shake. *But, what was I supposed to do?* I was a twenty-year-old man who had nowhere to go and no help!

Right before we moved in, my faith was challenged. Since I was out of work, I went many days without sufficient food, but God sustained me. After a while I was able to start receiving unemployment benefits. It was not much, but I was able to buy a little food to feed me from week to week. One day, I asked my mother to take me to the Employment Security Commission in Kinston, NC and she didn't want to do it. All the way to Kinston she complained and cursed at me and finally told me that she would not return for me. I would either have to call someone else, or walk back home.

I remember thinking, "What was I supposed to do?" I went in and applied for several jobs and once I was finished, I started walking and praying at the same time. I got a mile up the road and the Spirit of God spoke to me so plainly and said, "If you praise me before you get to the end of the road I will make away for you to have a ride." I said, "Ok, Lord. I will praise you!" I began to thank and praise God for what he was going to do and I walked another two or three miles with no ride. I was almost to the end of the road and still had no ride. I kept praising God and, lo and behold, I not only had a ride, but three people pulled up offering me a ride. One of the people that saw me walking was my sister. She drove to Kinston to take care of some business, not knowing she was going to run into me. God did what He said He was going to do.

Once again, the wonderful experiences with God were tempered with trouble. The demonic visitations started happening as soon as we settled into the house. I remember one night in particular, I felt this dark cold spirit in the room and my skin began to crawl and the hair stood up on my arms and head. This was a much stronger presence than I had ever experienced before. I immediately started praying, but this demon power wasn't going anywhere. I prayed for most of the night, pleading the blood of Jesus, and eventually I felt this spirit leave after many hours.

I finally fell asleep about three o'clock in the morning, but as soon as I drifted off to sleep, I heard the voice of God speak in my ear and say "Danny, get up and look out of the window." I remember waking up and saying, "Yes, Daddy." I got up and hit the blinds, but I didn't see anything so I went back to sleep. The next day I found out that the same time I looked out the blinds, some burglars had broken into my neighbor's house. Because they thought that I saw them, the burglars dropped the neighbor's stolen belongings and ran off. Even in the midst of what I was dealing with, God still showed He was the boss and that His power was greater than the demonic forces that were coming against me.

Just as I did before, I spent every night going into warfare with these demonic forces because they were tormenting me. It got to the point where I would rather sleep in my car than to be kept awake in the house, fighting demons. I would sneak out to the car when the streets were empty and in the mornings I would go back into the house before anyone saw me. I was embarrassed because it seemed I was a grown man, afraid to sleep in the house. The reality was, I just got tired of fighting every night.

Lessons from the Journey

With my grandfather's death, my mother's subsequent betrayal and the lack of support from others, it felt like the hurt just kept on coming! In time I have been able to forgive. Forgiveness is not for the offending party; forgiveness is for you so that you will not hinder the flow and blessings of God on your lives. Forgiveness is hard at times because we have the right to our feelings, but our feelings do not make it right. When we forgive, we release the burden of vengeance to God. The bible says in ***Romans 12:19, "Dearly beloved, avenge not yourselves, but rather give place unto wrath: for it is written, Vengeance is mine; I will repay, saith the Lord."*** God can deal with people in a way that we can't. When we deal with people who hurt us, the tendency is to hurt them in return, but worse. When God deals with them, He deals with their hurt so that eventually the persons involved will come back and apologize. This is all a part of the journey to the God-given promise. Sometimes on this journey we will be put in situations that seem to be very unfair, but it's all a part of the process. When we hold onto a person who has hurt us, we allow them to sit upon the throne of our heart and only God should inhabit that place!

Part IV

CHAPTER SIXTEEN

A New Aspect of Ministry

> *"Do not be surprised if there is an attack on your work, on you who are called to do it, on your innermost nature--the hidden person of the heart. The great thing is not to be surprised, nor to count it strange--for that plays into the hand of the enemy. Is it possible that anyone should set himself to exalt our beloved Lord and not instantly become a target for many arrows?"*[vii]

I was flourishing at my church. I had been there for over a year and was grounded in the word of God. In one service, my assistant pastor called for all the people who thought they may have healing ministries to come up to the front of the church so she could lay hands on them and stir up that gift. I was unsure, but my friend motioned for me to get in the line too. She laid hands on me but I must be honest, I didn't feel a thing. After the assistant pastor finished, she said to go and pray for someone that needed a healing.

I left the church that day and asked God to direct me to someone who needed His healing touch. The Lord led me to the home of my grandfather's cousin who I had not seen since my grandfather's death. Soon after I entered the house, two people ran out and started screaming, wondering who or what entered the house. They were my great cousin's daughter and son-in-law. They were in a closed room in the back of the house and rushed out after experiencing something alarming. They saw me and said, "When you walked in the house, the entire house started glowing." It was the glory of God that followed me in the house! I asked my grandfather's cousin how she was doing, not knowing that she could no longer walk without the assistance of a walker. I told her that I was there to pray for her and that God was going to heal her body. As I started praying for her I felt the power of God in a way that I never had before. Before I could get through praying for her, she started screaming, threw the walker down and started running through the house.

I witnessed a miracle! She ran back and forth through the house, screaming and praising God for what He had done. I remember leaving her house feeling ecstatic because after seeing so many demonic manifestations, I had witnessed the power God with my own eyes. At the next church service, I got up and shared the testimony of what I witnessed and the church was so excited that everyone started dancing and praising God. My confidence in my gift grew so I started witnessing about the power of God, praying for people continually and seeing the miraculous.

While this was going on, my mother started cursing my sister and me out because we were home when she wanted to entertain various married men. This happened with a particular gentleman, and my mother's berating was so awful that my sister said to me, "Junior, if I have to sleep on the street, I promise you that I will not stay here one more night." The next day she left and stayed with her boyfriend who eventually started beating her. My beautiful sister would fall victim to the same domestic violence that we witnessed my mother endure from her boyfriends. After that night I also left. I lived from house to house for months because I didn't want to be subjected to my mother's berating any longer. I began staying with one of my cousins in Greenville. God used that situation for me to start witnessing and telling people about Jesus. God was with me because I eventually had a group of ten guys that started coming to church with me. All ten of them gave their lives to the Lord!

One evening when we went into one of the roughest projects in Greenville to witness, a man came up to us and started arguing with me about the gospel of Jesus Christ. It wasn't the man, but rather it was Satan operating through him. The Holy Ghost rose up in me and before I knew it, I said, "Satan, the Lord rebuke you." The man immediately calmed down! It was the power of God and not me because in our own strength, we are no match for Satan. ***Ephesians 6:12 states, "For we wrestle not against flesh and blood, but against principalities, against powers, against the rulers of the darkness of this world, against spiritual wickedness in high places."*** So we are in a spiritual war and our battle is not with mere flesh and blood, but we are fighting unseen forces that cannot be fought with natural means. That night taught me that I had to stay in the presence of the Lord to always be full of the power of God. Satan is a real foe and as humans we do not have enough power within ourselves to deal with him and his demons.

I was able to get a machine operator job through a temp agency. It took some time to get used to shift work, but I adjusted pretty quickly. I went to work every day, worked very hard and God gave me great favor with the management. While working there I developed the name "plant evangelist." People would get nervous or anxious when they saw me coming because I loved God so much and everyone I came in contact with, I had to tell them about Jesus. Many souls were saved because of what God was doing through me.

While I was spreading the good news of the gospel, Satan was plotting to stop the movement. There was a particular young lady who took great interest in what I had to say. Honestly, because I was on a serious ego trip, I thought she was sincere. She acted like the heavens would open whenever I would speak, but it was all a ploy to bring me down. Sadly, I fell into the enemy's trap and had a sinful encounter with her. Satan humiliated me and I stained my witness, but God's grace is so amazing. I felt extremely ashamed, but I got back up!

When I had a couple of days off work, I went out with my friend who was an evangelist. We went into a very rough area, stood on the street corner and proclaimed the word of God with great boldness. My friend shared a powerful testimony of a time we pleaded with a young man, on several occasions, about giving his life to the Lord. Each time the young man would say he was not ready. We were all ready over two thousand years ago when Jesus hung his head and took the horrible beating that we so deserved. Jesus gave up all His royalty in heaven to walk as a man so He could die for our sins. So that is a lie from Satan that we are not ready!

Sadly, the young man got killed. My friend shared with the young men who were listening, that while he was in his study reading the bible, God opened his ears and allowed him to hear this young man screaming from hell. On that street corner, my friend gave a demonstration of how that young man sounded. The people were so horrified by the scream that some dropped the plates and glasses they held, allowing them to shatter on the ground. That night at least ten young men gave their lives to the Lord.

Lessons from the Journey

When Satan tries to bring a man or woman of God down, he often comes as an angel of light, presenting himself to be very innocent. Believe when I say I give him no glory, but the fact of the matter is that he is real and his attacks are real, with every attempt in mind to bring us down as believers. I am nothing within my own ability, but I can do all things through Christ who gives me the strength. Satan is a defeated foe, but that does not stop him from trying to bring distractions and trouble our way. Every chance he gets he will try to set us up to fall and eventually walk away from God.

Whenever there is a great anointing and purpose on your life and Satan has some idea that you have the potential to rattle his kingdom, he will bring strong, but subtle attacks against you. It will seem so innocent, but on the backside of it is sure destruction. He often uses your weaknesses as the avenue to bring you down. Yes, your weaknesses! Let's be real, Satan is a strategist and he has demons that are assigned to your life that follow you around and record your every action. These demonic hordes report back to Satan and he gives them the plan to bring you down, or at least try. The bible says in ***Isaiah 54:17, "No weapon that is formed against thee shall prosper; and every tongue that shall rise against thee in judgment thou shall condemn, this is the heritage of the servants of the Lord, and their righteousness is of me, saith the Lord."*** God never said that the weapon wouldn't form, but he promised that it would not prosper or be successful. I fell into sin and almost from the grace of God. Sin will take you further than you want to go and hold you longer than you can imagine.

CHAPTER SEVENTEEN

A Date with Destiny

> Hebrews 12:1 *"Wherefore seeing we also are compassed about with so great a cloud of witnesses, let us lay aside every weight and the sin which doth so easily beset us"*

After evangelizing on the street corner, we went to the house of one of the young men that had just accepted Christ. A car stopped by and a young lady came inside the house while two other women stayed in the car, and one of them seemed to be very intoxicated. I saw her and didn't think anything of it, not knowing that she would later become my wife. About three months later my friend and I took the young men to the aquatics center to hang out. While I was talking to one of them, I asked him if his girlfriend had any saved friends. He thought for a moment and told me that her sister just gave her life to the Lord and was looking for a man who had done the same. I expressed to him that I would love to meet her.

A month later he called me and said, "Man, I have not forgotten about you. What are you doing tomorrow?" I told him I had to work from 7am – 3pm and then I was free. The next day, I picked him up and we went to his girlfriend's house so I could be introduced to her sister. After a quick introduction, the four of us went to McDonald's on a double date so Sylvia and I could get better acquainted. I often hear people say "love at first sight" and this was one of those situations. We talked for hours and it seemed as if I had known Sylvia my entire life. I was able to open up to this lady, whom I had just met, and felt very comfortable doing so!

During our conversation, it was easy to tell her all about my weaknesses and unexpectedly, she didn't judge me. I had finally met someone who looked at me as a man of God, despite my struggles. Oh, the conversation was delightful and we both didn't want it to end! We left McDonald's after about four hours of conversing and I felt very optimistic about this relationship. We exchanged phone numbers and said our goodbyes. I went to work that night and I felt like an angel touched me! Sylvia was perfect in my eyes, although no one is perfect, but I felt like I had met my God-ordained wife. We went out on many dates and I always tried to be the perfect gentleman; but to my amazement, my girlfriend was not used to a man who complimented her, opened her door, and was at her every beck and call. As a result, we argued over simple things. It seemed that my angel had become a fallen angel.

Sadly, we decided to go our separate ways for a while. We both believed that if it were meant to be, we would come back together. She started coming to church with her godmother and there was one night when the co-pastor called her out for prayer. Sylvia received a word of prophecy that God was going to send her a good husband. *I could have died right then!* My heart dropped. I had let go of the one woman that I truly loved. After church that night I went to her house to try and reconcile with her, but she wasn't hearing anything I had to say. When I left there, my heart was so heavy and I cried for days because I thought I missed my appointment with my purpose.

For weeks I was sad. I would see Sylvia at church and try talking to her, but she would ignore me. One day while I was at work, a friend, who was also an older minister, began to talk to me about my situation with Sylvia. He heard me out and said, "Brother, she is playing mind games with you and she wants you to chase her." He told me how to turn the tables and get her attention. I did what he told me to do and guess what? It worked! One evening the phone rang, and to my surprise, it was Sylvia. She said, "I need to ask you a question." I coolly told her to go ahead (I didn't want her to know that I was excited about her phone call). Sylvia went on to ask, "Why is it you can talk to me on the phone, but say nothing to me in church?" The next day I went to work and told my friend what happened and he said, "I told you."

After that, we would speak more frequently. I called her from work one day and after we spoke for an hour, she invited me to her family's house for Thanksgiving dinner. It was a nice dinner and her sister-in-law's mother asked Sylvia, "So when are y'all getting married?" Sylvia gave a smirk and said, "We don't know right now." The next night I took her to church and we sat behind the guest speaker, who was a prophet. She turned around and asked me, "Is this your girlfriend?" I told her yes. She took our hands and put them together and said, "Stick with her, she is beautiful." What I didn't know is that she saw our purpose in the kingdom and that God was going to use us one day.

Sylvia and I started spending a lot time together and we did not do enough to uphold holiness in our relationship. Sylvia and I fell into sexual sin and a baby was conceived. According to **Psalm 139:2 *"thou knoweth my downsittng and mine uprising, thou understands my thought afar off."*** God knew that my wife and I were going to fall, but did that change his mind about us? No! When we fall into sin, God's grace is extended to us, but even though His grace is extended, that does not give us the right to continue in our sin. We chose to go ahead and get married as a result, because we wanted to please God more than anything!

During this time, I was still living with my mother. Two weeks prior to my wedding, I was sitting quietly in a room in the back of the house when I heard arguing coming from somewhere in the front. I jumped up and ran to the front door and when I looked out, I was appalled to see that my mother's married boyfriend was fussing and cursing her out. I immediately walked over to the car and asked my mother if she was okay and she replied, "Yes, I am okay, go in the house." I accepted her response but then her boyfriend got angry and asked, "What do you mean is she okay?" We began to exchange words and I said to him, "You need to calm down because you are in my neck of the woods." Immediately, he calmed down and I went back into the house and answered a call from one of my friends. While I was on the phone, my mother violently pushed the door open and began to curse me out.

My mother's explanation was that I'd made her married boyfriend even more upset with her. My friend asked if everything was okay and I said, "Yes." I hung up the phone and told my mother she would never have to worry about me intervening in her business again and I really didn't care what happened to her from that point on. Day after day, when she would come home, she would curse me out because of what happened that day. Finally, the day I got married I met her at the door and said to her, before she could mumble one curse word, "Before you start cursing, I will be moving out of your house very soon." My mother was spellbound and at a loss for words. She went to her room with her head hung down like she had lost her best friend. After about an hour, or so, she came in the room and said, "Whatever you need, you can take it." My reply was, "Okay, but no, thank you."

No one in the family, except my in-laws, had a clue that we were going to get married. I will never forget the morning that we went to the Justice of the Peace. Sylvia's parents accompanied us to be our two witnesses. My father-in-law asked me to step into the kitchen to have *'the talk'* each father has with the man about to marry his daughter. He said to me, "Danny, if you cannot take care of her, or if you have to beat on her, bring her back home!" "Wow", I thought, "brief and straight to the point!" But I understood that he meant business. On March 3, 1995, we became one in the eyes of God. Afterwards one of my friends allowed us to keep his car all day to have something really nice to ride around in after our big moment. We didn't have much to do but we were happy.

While riding around, enjoying one another, I decided to go to my house and tell my mother what we had done. We walked in the house and I was straight to the point! I said mom, "Meet your daughter-in-law." My mother was again speechless because I was proving to her that I could make it on my own. My mother was not happy for me at all and she just said, "Ok", not even a "congratulations" or "welcome" to my wife. So after that we left and went to view our apartment and go and pick out some furniture. Finally, after three weeks we moved into our first apartment together. It felt really good to be out on my own and away from all the negativity surrounding my mother and her immoral relationship. Our first night there my wife cooked me a meal fit for a king. We had steak, steak fries, and broccoli with cheese.

Lessons from the Journey

Our glimpse of David's path isn't one of perfection. David faltered. David sinned against the Lord in a major way when he shamefully took Uriah's wife and murdered him to cover his sin. Glory be unto God, this did not nullify the promises of God for David's life! And in Psalm 51, we see David's humility and honesty in confessing and repenting. The bible says in ***1 Corinthians 10:13 "No temptation has overtaken you but such as is common to man; and God is faithful, who will not allow you to be*** *tempted beyond what you are able, but with the temptation will provide the way of escape also, so that you will be able to endure it."* When we are tempted like David was, we have a guaranteed way of escape! Also, for the times when we do sin, God does not forsake us. But when we do sin, we can come boldly before the throne of God with a repentant heart. ***1 John 2:1 tells us we have an advocate with the Father through Jesus Christ!***

I want to encourage Christian singles who are dating, do not ever think that you are strong enough, even in the Lord, that you will not fall into sin. I do not care who you are, spending too much time alone as a Christian single with the opposite sex will lead to a fall. We all want someone to love and to call our own, but there is a way to date to keep both parties in a holy stance.

I believe what the bible says in ***Hebrews 12:14 "follow peace with all men, and holiness, without which no man shall see the Lord."*** God requires all of us to be holy as He is holy. Even our mistakes are in the plan of God! God knows what we are going to do before we do it.

CHAPTER EIGHTEEN

Settling Into Marriage

> *"Battles are fought in our minds every day. When we begin to feel the battle is just too difficult and want to give up, we must choose to resist negative thoughts and be determined to rise above our problems. We must decide that we're not going to quit. When we're bombarded with doubts and fears, we must take a stand and say: I'll never give up! God's on my side. He loves me, and He's helping me! I'm going to make it!"*[viii]

For the first month things were going well in our marriage until my insecurities started sprouting. They stemmed from the wrong expectations I had of women. The ones I got from my mother, having only seen her in multiple relationships and never being faithful to one. It was easy to project her disloyal behavior unto my wife, even though Sylvia did nothing to deserve it. When the real "me" came out, my wife got tired really quickly because I was possessive, controlling, and I had to know her every move. My behavior would almost destroy what God had ordained to be, but thanks to God my wife didn't give up on me. My wife saw something in me that enabled her to press past my insecurities and love me with an incomprehensible love.

However, even the most loving and forgiving person has a breaking point. I drove my wife to the point that she wanted out of the marriage and I still remember the night that she packed all of her clothes to leave. While she was packing in the bedroom, I ran in the living room to call my co-pastor. I hoped she would talk to Sylvia and could convince her to stay. After about ten minutes of pleading with my wife, she finally spoke with my co-pastor who was able to calm her down enough that she unpacked and stayed.

Jesus said in **Matthew 15:11 *"Not that which goeth into the mouth defiles a man; but that which cometh out of the mouth, this defiles a man."*** It is the hidden matters of the heart and mind that can ultimately destroy or alter our destiny. I knew I was insecure, but I had no idea that I was that bad. God allowed the trouble to come to show me what was in my heart and mind. It taught me that when these things come up out of you, the best thing to do is to deal with them right away because unresolved anger and hurt can be the silent killer to our destiny.

During the next couple of months things started getting tough because my job started having a lot of layoffs. I was barely getting 20 hours per week and the bills were piling up fast. We went without food but God sustained us, even in the midst of this difficult season. One morning I was awakened by the Holy Spirit to just get into prayer and the word of God, not knowing that things were getting ready to go from bad to worse. I went to work and they told everyone that we would be laid off indefinitely. At this point I was down in the dumps and I didn't know what to do because I had my light bill, phone bill, car payment, and rent. After falling two months behind on my rent, we received an eviction notice. *Can you imagine having two kids and a wife to take care of and nowhere to live?*

We had to do something and do it quickly, because if not, we would have to sleep in our car and it was extremely cold. God made a way as He always does! One of my wife's brothers allowed us to live with him and his family. At the time he had a doublewide mobile home and we stayed in one of the smaller rooms. My wife, my two children and I were cramped up in this small room that only had a small bed. My wife and I slept on the bed while we created a makeshift bed for my two babies because they were so small and we didn't want them to roll off the bed and hurt themselves. For the first month things were okay until the repo man figured out where we were and collected our car. It was close to income tax season so we were able to purchase a small car after receiving our tax refund.

The pressure started to get to us after a while. My wife and I were arguing more often and things seemed hopeless. One day while we were arguing, my wife got tired of quarreling and turned away from me. I sat on the edge of the bed and started talking to God. The Holy Spirit told me something that changed my way of thinking about marriage. The Holy Spirit asked me a question, "Do you know why your wife does not love you the way that you want her to?" I responded, "No. I don't, Lord." In that small, still voice, God said to me, "Because you don't love Me the way that you should." He went on to say, "The way you love Me is the way your wife loves you. You reflect My image and your wife reflects yours." I felt smaller than an ant at that moment because my relationship with God would ultimately dictate how I would treat my wife and what she would reciprocate back to me.

For six months we moved from house to house and we had to sleep in our car on occasion. It was rough and I often wanted to give up, but I had to think about more than just my feelings - I had a family that was depending on me. After about five months, I swallowed my pride and asked my mother if we could live there temporarily. She grudgingly agreed. We placed our furniture in storage until our living and job situation improved, but we were late on the storage bill too. We finally saved enough money to pay our storage bill, but when we gave the manager our name, the next thing he said added insult to injury. The manager said, "Y'all are one day too late because I sold all of your belongings yesterday." At that moment it seemed as if time stood still and everything was moving in slow motion.

All of our earthly belongings, except for a few clothes that we carried around with us, were gone! My wife and I were so heart-broken; we both cried. All of my pictures and my grandfather's things, which I kept for sentimental reasons, were gone. We left there with our heads hung down and our hearts devastated that such a horrific thing had happened to us.

After experiencing this I just *knew* that God forgot about us, but it was quite the contrary, God was setting us up for a great breakthrough. My job called me back to work and things seemed like they were about to turn in our favor. I went to work and for a month work was steady and I was starting to feel optimistic. Unfortunately, it didn't take too long for me to realize the inequality that was happening there. I endured personal experiences where coworkers were given preferential treatment over me in similar circumstances.

Overall, the blacks were mistreated and all the whites were given the opportunity to work the machines that ran all year long. One night I came in to work and was told that the head manager wanted me to meet him in the HR manager's office. This racist head manager told the HR manager he wanted me gone and if I walked in one second late, he would fire me. The HR manager didn't agree with him, so he said, "Danny would you rather take a permanent lay off?" I was in a bad position. If I didn't take it I would risk being fired; while on the other hand, if I took the layoff, I wouldn't be able to pay my bills.

Finally, I decided to accept the layoff. I called my wife and told her what was going on and she said to me, "Honey, it's going to be ok. God is going to work things out." It was a long drive from Farmville back to Greenville and I believe I cried all the way there. Sadly, it was a week before Thanksgiving and I had no idea how I was going to take care of my family. We had finally found somewhere to live, but because all of our belongings were gone, we had no furniture and slept on the floor. During this time my wife landed a job at Food Lion, a local supermarket, at night. We had very little money for gasoline, so I would take my wife to work and the kids and I would sleep in the car.

This went on for a couple months and it was tough, but it was a part of the process of God getting us to our promised place. As soon as the month of February came around, I received a phone call for an interview from a very good paying job. When the time came for my interview, my wife laid hands on my head and prayed that God would give me wisdom and favor. God did just that! I was hired after three interviews. I went to church happy and praising God that He had opened such a door for me and I told my wife she could leave the job at Food Lion because the management was being nasty to her.

After two weeks of training and orientation, I went to work for a lumber mill. I was on the cleanup crew and we shoveled sawdust all day long. *It didn't matter to me!* I could have shoveled cow manure and I would have been happy because now I could provide for my family. After six months, a position became open in the drying department. I had driven a forklift before but not anything so humungous. The forklifts had the capacity to carry two people in the cab and could lift up to 40,000 pounds. I was scared and I did make a mess. After about two months I was handling things well, so my supervisor moved me to pulling lumber off the green mill line. Believe me, each of these jobs had their challenges, but I was determined that I was going to be one of the best. Day after day when it was time to work my shift, I worked harder than everyone else. Eventually this would pay off because not only did I learn the forklift jobs, but I also learned the lead position job. God gave me unexplainable favor and I was chosen over operators that had years of experience over me for the lead position.

Lessons from the Journey

In the process of moving toward your God ordained place in life, there are times that God will allow trouble to come into our lives to purge out our hearts. Many times the deep-rooted things come from difficult situations and sadly the bulk of our hurt is inflicted during our childhood years. As children we do not ask to be born into this world nor do we choose our parents; God is the author and finisher of both our faith and life. God had a blueprint of our life before we were ever conceived in our mothers' wombs and he knows what it will take to get us to the God-given promises that he has over our lives.

After the Holy Spirit spoke those life-changing words to me concerning my marriage, I went to work on myself. So many times we want to point the finger at others when things go wrong, but I have learned that most of the time the issue lies within me. With God's help I have worked on this area, knowing that our ministry together is a part of God's purpose for my life.

The journey to our promise will not be easy, but the bible promises in **Galatians 6:9, "And let us not be weary in well doing: for in due season we shall reap, if we faint not."** It is in that moment that we feel weary that God is about to release heaven's best into our lives. The toughest part of the battle is always at the point of victory! I have experienced this so many times and I have also learned that if we do not pass the test the first time we will see it again.

CHAPTER NINETEEN

When the Storms Rise

> *Romans 5:3-5 "And not only so, but we glory in tribulations also: knowing that tribulation worketh patience; And patience, experience; and experience, hope; And hope maketh not ashamed; because the love of God is shed abroad in our hearts by the Holy Ghost which is given unto us."*

One shift, we stacked 15,000-pound weights on top of the wood in preparation for an impending hurricane. When I got home that night, we packed clothes so we could stay with my mother-in-law. Our mobile home wasn't a safe structure for such a storm. Before we left, I called my wife and children into the living room for prayer. I prayed and asked God to protect our belongings and us. We left, not knowing what would be the outcome once this massive storm came on land.

Hurricane Floyd proved to be the storm of the century! Again, we lost everything. After the storm, we couldn't get home for about 3-4 weeks and we were frustrated, but we were not alone. Hundreds of people were displaced from their homes. When the floodwaters finally receded and we were allowed to go home, our home had been condemned. The floodwaters damaged the walls and the floors. As a result, we had to apply for help from FEMA and the Red Cross. We had insurance, but it was only enough to pay off the loan and not enough to cover either a new place or other things we had lost. We were forced to find shelter so a couple from our church allowed us to live with them until we found somewhere else.

After several months passed, the couple we were living with started having marital issues so we had to move again. We were able to move into a house owned by our former church. There were other families that resided in the home also. Even though it was a fairly large home, it was still pretty crowded. After a couple months of us living in the church's house, one of the couples living there started having marital issues also. Again we were forced to move and, thankfully, we were able to find our own apartment. We moved out just as quickly as we could because we didn't want to be caught in the crossfire. Even though we were in our own apartment, we remember the promise that God had given us that He was going to bless us with our own home. However, we had no idea that the promise He had given us was going to have so many problems associated with it.

Months had gone by since we moved into our apartment and it seemed as if the promise that God had given us concerning home ownership was not going to happen, but we continued to stand on the promise! Finally, we had been approved for some funds that we didn't have to pay back to purchase our new home. However, we weren't aware of the stipulations associated with it. The agreement was that we had to purchase something comparable to what we had lost and that was a mobile home.

We were shocked and felt that it shouldn't matter, but my wife, who is strong in faith, said to me, "Honey, that's not what God promised us." We went to God in prayer and reminded Him of what He said. A month went by and nothing changed, but we didn't back down in our faith. Finally, after a couple months we received a phone call and the gentleman stated that we could take the funds and put it down on whatever we liked. But he said, "Be wise and find something that is affordable to your budget." *We did just that!* We asked our co-pastor to come with us so we could show her the house that we found, but when she saw it, she said, "This is not it." We were disappointed because our heart was set on that particular house, but we trusted her judgment.

Again, we went searching for a house and came across a brand new home. So we asked her again to come with us and she said, "This is it!" We contacted the realtor and started the process and because we obeyed the voice of God in our leader, the process went very smoothly for us.

The day had finally come that we were to close and I was very nervous. There were so many papers to sign that I got a headache. We finished and were given the keys to our brand new home. Even though we had so many obstacles, we stood on the promise that God had given us and He blessed us!

My wife, kids, and I were so ecstatic that we had somewhere that we could finally call our own. Once we moved in, it was months before the excitement wore off.

Lessons from the Journey

I have learned that storms in life are going to come, but if you weather the storm things will get better. Often, storms of life get the roughest and the darkest when we are at the point of a break through. We have to prepare for the storms of life through prayer and study of God's word.

Jesus said in **Matthew 4:4 "But he answered and said, it is written, Man shall not live by bread alone, but by every word that proceedeth out of the mouth of God."** The word that you receive in your spirit today may be the word you need to guide you through your next test. When we receive a direct promise from God, he also releases the necessary trouble to bring the promise to pass. Just as sure as the sun shines, that is how sure I am that we all have cloudy days. According to **Psalms 34:19 "Many are the afflictions of the righteous: but the Lord delivereth him out of them all."** Yes we have great promises from God, but He also promised us that we would have many problems.

CHAPTER TWENTY

Problems with Posterity

> *"Are we weak and heavy laden, cumbered with a load of care? Precious Savior, still our refuge, take it to the Lord in prayer. Do your friends despise, forsake you? Take it to the Lord in prayer! In His arms He'll take and shield you; you will find a solace there."*[ix]

My wife and I felt the need to become foster parents. We went through all the necessary trainings to become therapeutic foster parents and shortly after receiving our certifications we got our first children. Sadly, their mother dropped them off at the local Department of Social Services and told them she would return, but never did. The children were brother and sister and they immediately meshed very well with our family. We loved them as if they were our own children and after a few months they became very attached to us and started calling us mom and dad.

The kids stayed with us for about two years and we were presented with the option of adopting, but at that time we were not ready to adopt. The company's director became angry and set out to terminate our license. The company stated that they do not pressure their parents to adopt, but that wasn't true. So, after three months we received a phone call from our case manager stating that there was a problem with our sliding patio doors. My response was, "Please stop lying. What is the real issue?" She went on to say that she and the director would arrive at our home in about thirty minutes to discuss the matter. The problem was that we did not even have sliding patio doors! Once the team arrived at our home, they laid out their claims that would ultimately lead to us losing our license with this company.

We were so hurt and devastated by what had happened. They set us up and removed our foster children with the assistance of one the ladies from our former church. We could deal with the company and their deceit, but someone from our church joining in on the deception was too much.

It took us over a year to finally get over the pain of losing our foster children. We had to forgive the sister in the church that joined in on this hurtful situation. It's easier to forgive people who are not connected to you, but it is very difficult when it's people who are supposed to have the same mind and spirit. After two years passed, we decided to go back into foster care. We went with an awesome company that is very reputable.

While we were pursuing this, our birth kids were going to school and starting to hang around other children that were negative influences on them. I didn't know how I could help other children when my own children were in need of my attention and care. My middle son was, and still is, one of the brightest young men that I have had the privilege of knowing, but he was prone to stupid choices. He was the child that kept my wife and me praying. For two years we pulled him out of public schools and home schooled him so that we could try and help him build some type of tolerance to foolishness. After the two years passed we allowed him to enter back into the public school system. He did very well for a while, but ended up gravitating towards the wrong crowd again. We had to move him from one school to another within the county to try and keep him out of trouble. Even with the moves, we had one issue after another.

Eventually my son found football, and it was something that he enjoyed and it seemed to be a way out. His skills as a running back were phenomenal! Sadly, he ultimately fell in with the wrong crowd again. A promising career in football was replaced with a life that was not godly. We received phone calls from his school at least once or twice every two days. One day we received a phone call that he had come into the school smelling like marijuana. He was suspended and we had the task of getting him to tell the school resource officer where he got it. We spent about an hour talking and scolding him until he finally broke. His struggles reminded me of some of the things I went through as a teenager and I did not want him to follow such a difficult road.

While we were dealing with these situations, my oldest son, who did not live with us, needed my attention too. He would come over and we enjoyed his presence, but every time he was with us, my wife and I would argue badly.

We eventually went to my pastor for guidance. We learned it was a spiritual attack and only a time of separation would thwart the enemy's plan. It was a painful time for all of us, especially not being able to explain to him all that was happening.

Even though we were dealing with these issues, we still accepted foster kids into our home because these kids needed someone to help them. My wife received a phone call from another foster parent stating that she was tired of the young man that was residing in her home and wanted to know if we would take him. She went on to say that she was having marital issues and right then wasn't a good time for him to be in their home. The lady knew her husband would not go for removing him so she came up with a plan to have him removed by placing the blame on DSS. The child came into our home and for a couple of weeks we were in the "honeymoon stage," so he was perfect. He was respectful and helpful until I had to correct him and he became very angry. It took some time for him to calm down but he eventually did. I felt that foster care was a way for me to give back to God because of the way I grew up as a child. As I have stated, people who were no blood relation to me took me in, loved me as their own and raised me.

After being with us for a year, this young man's behavior had improved tremendously. One day he came home, was very irritable, and for no reason that we could figure out, just exploded in anger. After he calmed down I had a long talk with him and he told me that his former foster father had been going to the boys and girls club to see him without our knowledge. He told me the family wanted to adopt him, but it was all a ploy to get him back into their home so they could get income for taking care of him. The family knew they had no intention of adopting him.

He started misbehaving terribly; in fact, he once obtained a knife from someone and took it to school. He was suspended for ten days pending a meeting with the school board. While he was suspended, I had to leave him with my wife for a little while at her place of business. While there, my wife allowed him to use the restroom. He ran out the back door and around the corner where the former foster parent was awaiting for him to join them. The head of the agency, at the time, went along with this because they both worked in the same field and they had all conspired together. In the end he went back to the family, and we even see God's hand in that considering the other problems we were facing.

One night while I was sleeping I had an out-of-body experience. I drifted off to sleep, but then I woke up standing at the foot of my bed, while looking at my physical body lying on the bed. I remember seeing a very ugly demon walk in the room and he asked me, "Can I have your son?" Again he asked, "Can I have your son?" I remember saying, "No, you cannot have him!" I was standing there talking to a demon and I could see my wife trying to wake my body up, and my lips were moving but an unknown tongue was coming out. I finally went back into my body and I awoke, sat up, and told my wife what was going on and we immediately went into my son's room and talked with him.

Later that week we found out that my son was involved with some bad guys, but we also learned that he was asked to do something that he refused and there were some threats made against him, but God shielded him. My son called us after this visitation from the demon and told us about his predicament and that he didn't know what to do. We immediately told him that everything was going to be okay. *God will always send a warning before destruction comes.* We prayed and prayed that everything would work out and for God's protection for our family. God worked it out and my son graduated from high school unharmed!

Lesson from the Journey

I want to take the time and encourage someone that has been hurt by church folks; don't walk away from God. He didn't do it. When we don't forgive the people who hurt us, we are held hostage by our own feelings and the person sits on the throne of your heart. Unforgiveness acts as a cancer to the spirit and soul eating away at your life. It would have been easy for David to be bitter against his own son, Absalom, and retaliate for the betrayal and all the wrong done to him. Instead, he poured out his anger and hurt to God and let God take care of it!

Psalm 3:1-6 Lord, how many are my foes! How many rise up against me! Many are saying of me, "God will not deliver him." But you, Lord, are a shield around me, my glory, the One who lifts my head high. I call out to the Lord, and he answers me from his holy mountain. I lie down and sleep; I wake again, because the Lord sustains me. I will not fear though tens of thousands assail me on every side.

CHAPTER TWENTY-ONE

Walking in Purpose

> "Our cause is never more in danger than when a human, no longer desiring, but still intending, to do our Enemy's [God's] will, looks round upon a universe from which every trace of Him [God] seems to have vanished, and asks why he has been forsaken, and still obeys."[ix]

Three years before I was without a job, I was at a local restaurant and a man approached me and said, "God said don't worry about how and why your job gets rid of you, but know that God has a work for you to do." Guess what? Three years to the date, my job terminated my position because I went out on disability leave. I have been out of work for over six years now and God has provided. Not, only that, but God did have something for me to do – and I could not have imagined the way the enemy was going to try and stop God's plans.

In 2012 I decided that I was going to step out and start my evangelistic ministry. I went to my pastor and went through all the proper channels that were set up for ministers before they could go out and preach. I called the pastor and she gave me wisdom and told me that she would, that Sunday, lay hands on me to send me out. When Sunday came she wouldn't lay hands on me because she claimed she had no virtue. I wanted to fall down and cry because I was waiting for that moment! *How could she do that to me?* I left heartbroken that day, but I still trusted God!

My wife and I went to Maryland and God met us there. People were delivered, set free, healed, and filled with the Holy Ghost. When service was over I called my pastor and told her what God had done and she pretended to be happy. After we returned to North Carolina a week later, she called for an emergency 5AM prayer. I thought it was for the leadership, but I didn't know I was walking into a "tell off Danny" session. The pastor said, in front of everyone, that all that I did, or allowed God to do didn't mean anything to God. She went on to say my work was going to be burned, and that I was disobedient. My wife and I got up and walked out because I refused to be torn down and insulted like that. I gave that situation over to God and left it alone. As time passed, I was again *sat down*[xi] from ministering in the church.

Shortly after, my wife and I were invited to a prophetic service in Raleigh, NC. A prophet called my wife and I out to pray for us and said, "I am not an apostle, but God told me to lay hands on you and release you into full-time ministry." We took that word of prophecy very lightly and went back to our comfort zone. A few months later, God allowed Satan to come in and cause havoc, pushing us out of our comfortable place where we had served for twenty years. We were treated like castaways by our church family and were gossiped about by the pastor we held so dear to our hearts. We left the ministry heart-broken and adrift, but I knew what God had promised to me.

We found ourselves bitter for a while and through our new journey we ended up in a church in Rocky Mount, NC. The pastor there seemed to love us, but as time progressed, we found out quickly that was a front. After attending there for several months, my former pastor called this pastor and told her that my wife was a witch. We were so hurt because even though we had been done wrong, we still loved our former pastor. Although this was hurtful, it wasn't surprising because we had seen them do this to others, but it was hard when we had to experience it for ourselves. We eventually left that church, too, because the pastor was preaching one thing and living another. We prayed and asked God to lead us to a church where there was a pastor who could see the destiny and purpose on our lives for ministry.

We ended up in another ministry where we thought we could fit and find our way to our God-given purpose. This pastor welcomed us in with open arms and told us everything we wanted to hear. We started serving right away because this pastor understood that we had served twenty years under a giant in the gospel and that pastor had imparted some good things in us. My wife warned me not to be so willing to help her because God had shown her that this pastor was only out to use me for her selfish gain and her love for us was all a front. The pastor saw we were chosen by God and tried to drain us and I got my feelings hurt again!

When we first went to this ministry, we were upfront and honest with this particular pastor that we believed God was calling us into full-time ministry. Her reply was, "I can see that on your life." We expressed to her that after a year we would start our bible study, then eventually transition into a full-blown ministry. After the year passed, we went back to her and reminded her of the conversation that we had from the beginning. The pastor expressed she remembered and that she would help us anyway she could. However, when the time came and we released our invitation on social media of our intentions, she became very angry! This began a series of events that led up to us walking away from this pastor who we thought would be our spiritual covering. Instead of us just having a bible study for six months to a year, we were forced to begin our Sunday services ahead of schedule.

On February 4, 2015 we began our first bible study and started Greater Judah Deliverance Ministry. It has been a great challenge, but it has been worth pursuing the will of God for our lives.

Lessons from the Journey

When God calls you into ministry you have to answer the call or He will, like an eagle, throw you out of the nest and you have two options: either fly or die. Sadly, when God has called you to do a work or to be a world changer for His glory, everyone will not be happy for you! As a matter of fact, you will find that some who were pushing you were actually hoping that you would give up and eventually throw in the towel.

Often the people that we look to for support and encouragement are our biggest haters. Too many times they see you in your present state of being and not in your God ordained future. In their mind you may still be like David - the little, ruddy lad, tending sheep - but they don't understand that God has already anointed you for greatness. I want to encourage you, while you are reading this, to step out into what God has placed within you because it's in that place you will find your ultimate fulfillment! It's rewarding when you are doing what God has placed you on earth to do.

Epilogue

> *Psalm 139:23-24 "Search me, O God, and know my heart: try me, and know my thoughts: And see if there be any wicked way in me, and lead me in the way everlasting."*

My life, my family, my story is not about perfection. It is about this rough journey that serves to bring about God's purpose and to build our character along the way. God is still teaching me and I wanted to share with you what I have learned so far. As I said in the beginning, that is why King David comes to mind when I think of someone anointed mightily by God, used greatly, blessed beyond belief, yet had a road that was also filled with a lot of sadness, mistakes, hurt, betrayal, and more. Through his experience we can see that even though we falter, our God is faithful. We also see clearly that the difficulty of the road, or what outsiders may have to say about our way, has nothing to do with the promises God has set before us! The journey is not easy and is not perfect, but it is worth it because God is worth it, and because His plan and purposes for us are definitely worth it!

Even though the demonic activity in my life has been great, I have learned as a pastor and as a child of the King, that I have authority over depression and oppression. **Luke 10:19 says *"Behold, I give unto you power to tread on serpents and scorpions, and over all the power of the enemy; and nothing shall by any means hurt you."*** We, as believers, have been given power over all the powers of the enemy and we have to choose to walk in our God given authority. It took me many years to come to realize this truth that I am free and I can stay free. It took my wife many years to get used to demonic activity trafficking through our home and life. Since we have transitioned into ministry, my wife seeks every opportunity to pray for someone who is oppressed by the devil to get him or her totally free.

Before I go, let me pray for you:
Father, in the name of Jesus I ask that every person who reads this book will be touched by the power of your Spirit! Father I pray in the name of Jesus that you open the eyes of their understanding that your people will see their God given purpose in the midst of their pain; I ask you to give them the grace necessary to get through each struggle victoriously and with a greater grace and anointing to accomplish your perfect will in Jesus' name Amen!

i.	Hymn, A Mighty Fortress is Our God, translated by Frederick Hedge; based on Psalm 46
ii.	Hymn, Count Your Blessings by Johnson Oatman
iii.	Where two or more dancers compete to determine who is the best
iv.	Black Spirits – An especially terrorizing type of demon
v.	Hymn, Til the Storm Passes By Mosie Lister
vi.	Quote by Chuck Swindoll
vii.	Quote by Amy Carmichael
viii.	Quote by Joyce Meyers
ix.	Hymn, What A Friend We Have in Jesus by Joseph Scriven
x.	Quote by C.S. Lewis "Screwtape Letters" pg.40
xi.	Sat Down – Term meaning a temporary suspension from serving in the church

ABOUT THE AUTHOR

Pastor Danny Gardner was raised by the late Queen Esther Gardner and Johnnie Thrower of Ayden, NC. He has a Bachelor's degree in Theology and an Associate's degree in Advertisement and Graphic Design.

Pastor Gardner received the Lord Jesus Christ as his Savior at the age of 20 and God dealt with him early in his walk with Christ about the calling that was on his life. God delivered him from great demonic possession and oppression, so this is why the passion burns in his heart to see God's people liberated from the powers of darkness. He has recently published his first book, "My Promise has a Problem," which is a memoir depicting his battles with demons and how God delivered him.

After 22 years of walking with the Lord, Pastor Gardner finally said yes to the call and founded Greater Judah Deliverance Ministry with his lovely wife, Co-Pastor Sylvia Gardner. Pastor and Co-Pastor Gardner have been married for 20 years and have three boys Michael, Naigel, and Dantrell. The couple has a tremendous passion for marriage ministry.

As the senior pastor of Greater Judah Deliverance Ministry, Pastor Gardner's mission is to fulfill the great commission by reaching the unsaved for the glory of God. He believes that through and by the name of Jesus Christ, captives can be set free, the blind can receive sight, and the oppressed can be delivered.

> *Matthew 10:1 And when he had called unto him his twelve disciples, he gave them power against unclean spirits, to cast them out, and to heal all manner of sickness and all manner of disease.*

Print copies of this book can be purchased from Rain Publishing and online bookstores.
www.rainpublishing.com

You can also mail your request to:

Please include the following with your order: Title, number of copies, shipping address, contact information, payment ($9.99 x # of copies) including shipping ($5.00), and mail to:

Danny Gardner/Rain Publishing PO Box 702
Knightdale, NC 27545

www.ingramcontent.com/pod-product-compliance
Lightning Source LLC
Chambersburg PA
CBHW070624300426
44113CB00010B/1651